VALERIE BROMANN

ADAMS MEDIA
NEW YORK LONDON TORONTO SYDNEY NEW DELHI

Adams Media
An Imprint of Simon & Schuster, Inc.
100 Technology Center Drive
Stoughton, Massachusetts 02072

First Adams Media trade paperback edition May 2023

Interior design by Colleen Cunningham
Interior images © Getty Images/calvindexter, A-Digit, isiddheshm, Panptys, Herba Mykhailo, Vadym Kalitnyk, Ondřej Pros, LysenkoAlexander, Sudowoodo, Grace Maina, Catur Nurhadi, Burhan Adiatma, Mark Astakhov, Artem Stepanov, Elena Mitrokhina, Ihor Reshetniak, DragonTiger, primulakat, Nadiinko, Ivan Zakalevych, -VICTOR-, 4ndrei, JakeOlimb, cveiv, Skarin, slalomp, Kolomiiets Iryna, Tatyana Nesterenko, arcady_31, CurrantCrescent; 123RF/Christophe Testi

Manufactured in the United States of America

1 2023

ISBN 978-1-5072-2043-6

Contents

Introduction

Road trips aren't about getting to your destination as fast as you can. They're about taking your time, pulling off the highway, and enjoying the drive. They're about taking those detours to explore small towns, giant roadside attractions, scenic overlooks, national parks, and places off the beaten path. They're about rolling down the windows, blasting your favorite playlist, having fun, and making lasting memories.

Whether you're driving down the East Coast on Route 1, across the country on Route 66, or up the Pacific Coast Highway, road trips can be life-changing adventures packed full of incredible sites and experiences—ones that you just don't get by taking a direct flight!

You'll never want to forget any of your favorite road trips. So record those memories and keep them alive long after your suitcase is unpacked with *The Road Trip Journal & Activity Book*! This book serves as both a travel diary and an entertainment guide, so you can keep track of your trip *and* be sure that no one is falling asleep at the wheel along the way. You'll find places to record information about each stretch of a longer road trip with a daily travel log, three journal prompts, and two road trip games or activities that will help pass the time between stops and bring everyone in the car closer together.

You'll find activities that will keep you and your travel companions entertained the whole way there (and back!), such as:

- Be the first to find everything on a road trip scavenger hunt (there must be a neon motel sign coming up!)
- Dare someone to eat a gas station hot dog
- Make up a "while you were napping" story to tell someone who nodded off

Each activity in the book can entertain both the driver and passengers so no one will be left asking, "Are we there yet?"

After your trip ends, *The Road Trip Journal & Activity Book* will make a lasting keepsake, so you'll never forget a moment of that girls' weekend, summer adventure, or couples' trip. Look back on every meal, attraction, and unforgettable memory as you dream about your next destination.

Ready to head out? Prep your car, gather your friends, and hit the road. And let this book be your backseat driver!

PART 1

On the Road

Every road trip is an adventure worth writing about! In this part of the book, you'll have the opportunity to log your travels, write about your trip, and have a little fun along the way. This part is divided into fifty (four-page) sections where you can keep track of an entire shorter trip or one stretch of a longer trip. In each section, you'll find a place to:

- **Record your itinerary:** Keep track of where you went, who drove, what the weather was like, and stops you planned to see by filling in the daily itineraries.
- **Respond to journal prompts:** Think about your initial impressions of the place you visited and what you were most excited to see, and answer a bonus prompt unique to that stretch.
- **Do fun activities:** For each stretch of the trip, you'll find two games, activities, or challenges that will keep everyone entertained in the car, during pit stops, or at the hotel. Some are short activities that are perfect to finish when traveling one particularly monotonous expanse of road, while others will keep you occupied throughout your entire journey as you check back to fill in lists or check off scavenger hunt items.

Whether you go through every page on one very long road trip or pick up this book again and again for every road trip you take, your group is sure to stave off boredom and have a blast. Plus, after you get home and unpack your luggage, you can take a look back at what you wrote and relive all the amazing memories you made along the way.

ROAD TRIP

STRETCH #:

DATE:

TO:

STARTING POINT:

ENDING POINT:

TODAY'S DRIVER(S):

WEATHER TODAY:

MUST-SEE STOPS

- [ ]
- [ ]
- [ ]
- [ ]
- [ ]
- [ ]

ITINERARY

MORNING:

AFTERNOON:

NIGHT:

What was our first impression of one of today's stops and how did it change by the time we left?

What were we most excited to see at one of today's stops and did it end up being our favorite part?

Why did we want to take this road trip?

TRAVEL NOTES

ROAD TRIP DREAMS

DATE:

Some travelers love to make stop after stop while others prefer to drive straight to their destination. Some travelers book everything ahead of time, and others play things by ear. How do you like to road trip? And what do you want to get out of your time on the road? Get a sense of what everyone's feeling by checking off what each traveler is hoping to experience on this road trip, and then create a few road trip resolutions that will help guide your journey.

On this road trip, I want to...	**NAME:**	**NAME:**	**NAME:**	**NAME:**
Have Fun	☐	☐	☐	☐
Learn Something New	☐	☐	☐	☐
Be Flexible	☐	☐	☐	☐
Enjoy Nature	☐	☐	☐	☐
Drive Straight There	☐	☐	☐	☐
Pamper Ourselves	☐	☐	☐	☐
Explore History	☐	☐	☐	☐
Leave Our Comfort Zone	☐	☐	☐	☐
Get Sun	☐	☐	☐	☐
Stay Up Late	☐	☐	☐	☐
Make Memories	☐	☐	☐	☐
Plan Ahead	☐	☐	☐	☐
Be Lazy	☐	☐	☐	☐
Get Going Early	☐	☐	☐	☐

Our Road Trip Resolutions:

THE HOT SEAT

Get to know your travel partners by putting them in the heated (hot) seat. Give everyone three minutes to answer rapid-fire questions about themselves. Use the road trip–friendly questions here or brainstorm your own.

DATE:

1. What is your favorite thing about road trips?
2. Who is your favorite road trip partner?
3. What are you most looking forward to about this trip?
4. What were you least looking forward to about this trip?
5. What was the best road trip you've ever taken?
6. What was the worst road trip you've ever taken?
7. What is your favorite type of travel accommodation?
8. What is your favorite roadside attraction?
9. What is your favorite country? State? City?
10. Where is the farthest place you ever traveled in a car?
11. If you could travel for one month, where would you go?
12. Where do you want to travel to next?
13.
14.
15.
16.
17.
18.
19.
20.

ROAD TRIP

STRETCH #:

DATE:

TO:

STARTING POINT:

ENDING POINT:

TODAY'S DRIVER(S):

WEATHER TODAY:

MUST-SEE STOPS

- [ ]
- [ ]
- [ ]
- [ ]
- [ ]
- [ ]

ITINERARY

MORNING:

AFTERNOON:

NIGHT:

What was our first impression of one of today's stops and how did it change by the time we left?

What were we most excited to see at one of today's stops and did it end up being our favorite part?

What is the best part about taking a road trip?

TRAVEL NOTES

DATE:

DESIGN YOUR DREAM CAR

What would your dream road trip car look like? Would it get you to your next destination at high speeds? Would it have features like automatic parking and driving? Would it come with unlimited trunk space to pack your whole closet in? Think about everything that would make your car the ultimate road trip vehicle and record your answers here.

Color: ____________________

Seats: ____________________

Steering wheel: ____________________

Trunk: ____________________

Wheels: ____________________

Inside design: ____________________

____

____

Outside design: ____________________

____

____

Features: ____________________

____

____

ROAD TRIP HASHTAG

DATE:

Commemorate your time together on the road by creating a unique road trip hashtag. Brainstorm ideas to create a tag that captures the spirit of your adventure. Think about: Who is in the car? Where are you going? Is there a theme to your road trip? A reason you're taking it? What year or season is it? Come up with a list of words that feel like they fit, try out a few combinations, and then choose the one everyone likes best! Be sure to use your hashtag every time you post about the trip so your friends can follow along and you have an archive to look back on.

KEY WORDS

HASHTAG IDEAS

FINAL HASHTAG

ROAD TRIP

STRETCH #:

DATE:

TO:

STARTING POINT:

ENDING POINT:

TODAY'S DRIVER(S):

WEATHER TODAY:

MUST-SEE STOPS

- [ ]
- [ ]
- [ ]
- [ ]
- [ ]
- [ ]

ITINERARY

MORNING:

AFTERNOON:

NIGHT:

What was our first impression of one of today's stops and how did it change by the time we left?

What were we most excited to see at one of today's stops and did it end up being our favorite part?

What traits make the perfect road trip partner?

TRAVEL NOTES

DATE:

TWO TRUTHS AND A LIE

This game lets you test just how much you know about your carmates. To play, each person takes a turn telling three things about themselves—but one of those things is completely untrue. Everyone else then has to guess which of the three "facts" is actually a lie. It's up to you to guess whether your friend really went storm chasing in Oklahoma, bungee jumping in Las Vegas, or white water rafting in West Virginia. Record everyone's answers and circle the one that turns out to be false.

Name:	**Name:**	**Name:**	**Name:**
Fact One:	Fact One:	Fact One:	Fact One:
Fact Two:	Fact Two:	Fact Two:	Fact Two:
Fact Three:	Fact Three:	Fact Three:	Fact Three:

ROAD TRIP TO-DO LIST

What are you most looking forward to doing on your road trip? Seeing the sights? Relaxing at the hotel? Feeling the freedom of the road? Whatever your favorite part of travel is, there are certain things that everyone should try to do at least once. Here are some ideas to add to your to-do list, but feel free to add your own ideas too. Check them all off as you go!

DATE:

- ☐ Try a local delicacy
- ☐ Swim in a hotel pool
- ☐ Take a group photo
- ☐ Take an unexpected detour
- ☐ Stop at a world's largest thing
- ☐ Take a hike
- ☐ Go through a drive-through
- ☐ See a national monument
- ☐ Pull over at a scenic overlook
- ☐ Stop for snacks
- ☐ Take a backseat nap
- ☐ Play a road trip game
- ☐ Visit a national park
- ☐ Watch a sunset or sunrise
- ☐ Buy souvenirs
- ☐ Stop at a welcome center
- ☐ Fill up the gas tank
- ☐ Sing along to the radio
- ☐ Explore a museum
- ☐ Visit a beach
- ☐ ....
- ☐ ....
- ☐ ....
- ☐ ....
- ☐ ....
- ☐ ....
- ☐ ....
- ☐ ....
- ☐ ....

ROAD TRIP

STRETCH #:

DATE:

TO:

STARTING POINT:

ENDING POINT:

TODAY'S DRIVER(S):

WEATHER TODAY:

MUST-SEE STOPS

☐

☐

☐

☐

☐

☐

ITINERARY

MORNING:

AFTERNOON:

NIGHT:

What was our first impression of one of today's stops and how did it change by the time we left?

What were we most excited to see at one of today's stops and did it end up being our favorite part?

What is the most memorable thing we saw from the car on this stretch?

TRAVEL NOTES

DATE:

GAS STATION SNACK CHALLENGE

Rev up your snacking game with this unusual food challenge. The next time you pull over at a gas station, have each person buy a snack for the car without knowing what everyone else chose. Assign each passenger a different category, like salty, sweet, hot, or beverage, and see what kind of options you end up with. The person who bought the item should taste and rate it, then share it with anyone else who wants to try a bite.

SALTY SNACK	BEVERAGE	BAKED GOOD
Item:	Item:	Item:
Player:	Player:	Player:
Rating: ☆ ☆ ☆ ☆ ☆	Rating: ☆ ☆ ☆ ☆ ☆	Rating: ☆ ☆ ☆ ☆ ☆
SWEET SNACK	**HOT ITEM**	**OTHER**
Item:	Item:	Item:
Player:	Player:	Player:
Rating: ☆ ☆ ☆ ☆ ☆	Rating: ☆ ☆ ☆ ☆ ☆	Rating: ☆ ☆ ☆ ☆ ☆

WHICH STATES HAVE YOU BEEN TO?

DATE:

There are fifty states in the US. How many have you been to? Check off the states you've visited, then compare your answers to see who has traveled to the most and who has some catching up to do.

Alabama
Alaska
Arizona
Arkansas
California
Colorado
Connecticut
Delaware
Florida
Georgia
Hawaii
Idaho
Illinois
Indiana
Iowa
Kansas
Kentucky
Louisiana
Maine
Maryland
Massachusetts
Michigan
Minnesota
Mississippi
Missouri
Montana
Nebraska
Nevada
New Hampshire
New Jersey
New Mexico
New York
North Carolina
North Dakota
Ohio
Oklahoma
Oregon
Pennsylvania
Rhode Island
South Carolina
South Dakota
Tennessee
Texas
Utah
Vermont
Virginia
Washington
West Virginia
Wisconsin
Wyoming

Passenger #1 Name: ______________________ Total: ______

Passenger #2 Name: ______________________ Total: ______

Passenger #3 Name: ______________________ Total: ______

Passenger #4 Name: ______________________ Total: ______

ROAD TRIP

STRETCH #:

DATE:

TO:

STARTING POINT:

ENDING POINT:

TODAY'S DRIVER(S):

WEATHER TODAY:

MUST-SEE STOPS

- [ ]
- [ ]
- [ ]
- [ ]
- [ ]
- [ ]

ITINERARY

MORNING:

AFTERNOON:

NIGHT:

What was our first impression of one of today's stops and how did it change by the time we left?

What were we most excited to see at one of today's stops and did it end up being our favorite part?

What other method of transportation for this trip would we choose and why?

TRAVEL NOTES

DATE:

UNIQUE PHOTO CHALLENGE

There are so many things to take photos of on a road trip that you'll surely fill up your phone storage with epic moments: group shots, glorious landscapes, world's largest things, monuments, and more. But don't forget to capture interesting little moments too. Use this list to curate a one-of-a-kind gallery of some of the details you might otherwise overlook.

- ☐ Luggage in the car trunk
- ☐ Reflection in the rearview mirror
- ☐ Everyone packed in the car
- ☐ Road sign for your destination
- ☐ Landscape through the car window
- ☐ Map of your route
- ☐ Favorite snack
- ☐ Close-up detail from an attraction
- ☐ Restaurant menu
- ☐ Shelf of souvenirs
- ☐ Postcard rack
- ☐ Filling up at gas station
- ☐ What you wore
- ☐ "Welcome to..." state or city sign
- ☐ Hotel lobby
- ☐ Morning coffee
- ☐ The road ahead
- ☐ Close-up of something in nature
- ☐ A page of this journal
- ☐ ______________
- ☐ ______________
- ☐ ______________
- ☐ ______________
- ☐ ______________
- ☐ ______________
- ☐ ______________
- ☐ ______________
- ☐ ______________
- ☐ ______________
- ☐ ______________
- ☐ ______________

THE ULTIMATE ROAD TRIP SOUNDTRACK

A well-curated soundtrack can provide the perfect background to a day behind the wheel. Just like in a movie when someone steps in to save the day or the two leads lean in for their first kiss, having the right song for the right moment can make or break the scene. Build your ultimate traveling soundtrack by finding the ideal song for some of the best moments of your day on the road.

DATE:

Song to start the morning:

Song for idyllic scenery:

Song to give you energy:

Song for a long stretch of road:

Song for a fun road trip stop:

Song that mentions your destination:

Songs that mention your name(s):

Song for a long hike:

Song for winding down:

ROAD TRIP

STRETCH #:

DATE:

TO:

STARTING POINT:

ENDING POINT:

TODAY'S DRIVER(S):

WEATHER TODAY:

MUST-SEE STOPS

- [ ]
- [ ]
- [ ]
- [ ]
- [ ]
- [ ]

ITINERARY

MORNING:

AFTERNOON:

NIGHT:

What was our first impression of one of today's stops and how did it change by the time we left?

What were we most excited to see at one of today's stops and did it end up being our favorite part?

If we could take a road trip with any famous person who would it be and why?

TRAVEL NOTES

DATE:

FANTASY ROAD TRIP

You might be taking the road trip of a lifetime—or you might just be trying to get where you're going. In either case, there's always room for a little improvement. Design your fantasy road trip: Where are you going? Who is coming? How are you getting there? What makes this your dream...and how can you make it a reality?

Names: ______________________

Vehicle: ______________________

Who is coming: ______________________

Starting point: ______________________

Special things you are packing: ______________________

Destination: ______________________

Length of trip: ______________________

Stops: ______________________

Why is this a fantasy road trip? ______________________

____

____

____

DESIGN A ROAD TRIP LOGO

Every good brand has a memorable logo—something that catches your eye, draws you in, and makes you want whatever the emblem is selling. Your road trip can have a logo too! Check out other logos you see along your drive and brainstorm one for your trip. What colors would it include? Would it be a single word or an artistic collage of the things you saw? Maybe an abstract symbol can capture the people and sights that stood out. Design a logo that represents your trip in the space here.

DATE:

ROAD TRIP

STRETCH #:

DATE:

TO:

STARTING POINT:

ENDING POINT:

TODAY'S DRIVER(S):

WEATHER TODAY:

MUST-SEE STOPS

- [ ]
- [ ]
- [ ]
- [ ]
- [ ]
- [ ]

ITINERARY

MORNING:

AFTERNOON:

NIGHT:

What was our first impression of one of today's stops and how did it change by the time we left?

What were we most excited to see at one of today's stops and did it end up being our favorite part?

Describe one place we spent the night in detail.

TRAVEL NOTES

DATE:

SPECIAL REQUESTS

What do you most look forward to when arriving at a hotel? A comfy mattress to sink into? A hot shower to wash away the day? A zoo of towel origami animals propped on the bed? When booking accommodations for the night, have a little fun with the special requests field. While normally used to ask for a dog-friendly room or an ocean view, let your imagination run wild. Request anything from extra pillows or a robe to a photo of your favorite celebrity on the nightstand, a dinosaur drawing left on the bed, or a pillow fort. See how many hotels you can get to comply with your weird requests!

Hotel: ____________________

Request: ____________________

Fulfilled: **Yes No** Rating: ☆ ☆ ☆ ☆ ☆

Hotel: ____________________

Request: ____________________

Fulfilled: **Yes No** Rating: ☆ ☆ ☆ ☆ ☆

Hotel: ____________________

Request: ____________________

Fulfilled: **Yes No** Rating: ☆ ☆ ☆ ☆ ☆

Hotel: ____________________

Request: ____________________

Fulfilled: **Yes No** Rating: ☆ ☆ ☆ ☆ ☆

MOST LIKELY TO...

We've all heard of senior superlatives—those yearbook pages that declare who in your class is the class clown, most artistic, or most likely to succeed. Shift gears and reimagine those classic class rankings as a car game. Take turns coming up with superlatives of your own. They can be a typical idea, like "most athletic"; something more personal, like "most likely to max out their credit card"; or something related to your trip, like "most likely to make a wrong turn." For every superlative, nominate passengers, then everyone in the car has to point to who they think is the most likely to hold that title.

DATE:

Superlative:

Nominated:

Winner:

Superlative:

Nominated:

Winner:

Superlative:

Nominated:

Winner:

Superlative:

Nominated:

Winner:

ROAD TRIP

STRETCH #:

DATE:

TO:

STARTING POINT:

ENDING POINT:

TODAY'S DRIVER(S):

WEATHER TODAY:

MUST-SEE STOPS

- ☐
- ☐
- ☐
- ☐
- ☐
- ☐

ITINERARY

MORNING:

AFTERNOON:

NIGHT:

What was our first impression of one of today's stops and how did it change by the time we left?

What were we most excited to see at one of today's stops and did it end up being our favorite part?

What did we eat on this road trip that was most delicious?

TRAVEL NOTES

FOOD FIGHT

Many cities are known for that one iconic food item. Chicago-style hot dogs, Philly cheesesteaks, Minneapolis Juicy Lucys, Buffalo wings—the list is endless! And, often, the list of places to eat that item is endless too! Are you traveling to a location known for its one must-have dish? Save room in your travel itinerary—and your stomach—to hop around town and sample it at two or more places. Taste-test the different versions and pit them against each other in a food fight. Rate each and see which interpretation you think comes out on top.

DATE:

Item: ______________________________

____

Version One: ______________________________

____

Notes: ______________________________

____

Rating: ☆ ☆ ☆ ☆ ☆

Version Two: ______________________________

____

Notes: ______________________________

____

Rating: ☆ ☆ ☆ ☆ ☆

Winner: ______________________________

____

Item: ______________________________

____

Version One: ______________________________

____

Notes: ______________________________

____

Rating: ☆ ☆ ☆ ☆ ☆

Version Two: ______________________________

____

Notes: ______________________________

____

Rating: ☆ ☆ ☆ ☆ ☆

Winner: ______________________________

____

LICENSE PLATE GAME

DATE:

The License Plate Game is a road trip classic and always an entertaining way to pass the time in the car. Keep your eyes peeled for cars sporting license plates from every state, province, or territory and check them off as you see them.

- ☐ Alabama
- ☐ Alaska
- ☐ Arizona
- ☐ Arkansas
- ☐ California
- ☐ Colorado
- ☐ Connecticut
- ☐ Delaware
- ☐ District of Columbia
- ☐ Florida
- ☐ Georgia
- ☐ Hawaii
- ☐ Idaho
- ☐ Illinois
- ☐ Indiana
- ☐ Iowa
- ☐ Kansas
- ☐ Kentucky
- ☐ Louisiana
- ☐ Maine
- ☐ Maryland
- ☐ Massachusetts
- ☐ Michigan
- ☐ Minnesota
- ☐ Mississippi
- ☐ Missouri
- ☐ Montana
- ☐ Nebraska
- ☐ Nevada
- ☐ New Hampshire
- ☐ New Jersey
- ☐ New Mexico
- ☐ New York
- ☐ North Carolina
- ☐ North Dakota
- ☐ Ohio
- ☐ Oklahoma
- ☐ Oregon
- ☐ Pennsylvania
- ☐ Rhode Island
- ☐ South Carolina
- ☐ South Dakota
- ☐ Tennessee
- ☐ Texas
- ☐ Utah
- ☐ Vermont
- ☐ Virginia
- ☐ Washington
- ☐ West Virginia
- ☐ Wisconsin
- ☐ Wyoming
- ☐ Alberta
- ☐ British Columbia
- ☐ Manitoba
- ☐ New Brunswick
- ☐ Newfoundland and Labrador
- ☐ Northwest Territories
- ☐ Nova Scotia
- ☐ Nunavut
- ☐ Ontario
- ☐ Prince Edward Island
- ☐ Quebec
- ☐ Saskatchewan
- ☐ Yukon

ROAD TRIP

STRETCH #: DATE:

TO:

STARTING POINT: ENDING POINT:

TODAY'S DRIVER(S):

WEATHER TODAY:

MUST-SEE STOPS

- ☐
- ☐
- ☐
- ☐
- ☐
- ☐

ITINERARY

MORNING:

AFTERNOON:

NIGHT:

What was our first impression of one of today's stops and how did it change by the time we left?

What were we most excited to see at one of today's stops and did it end up being our favorite part?

What is our favorite part of travel? Why?

TRAVEL NOTES

DATE:

ROAD TRIP WINS

Experiencing the open road and exploring the country is a win in itself, but what other wins have you encountered along the way? Whether it's making it to that late-night drive-in just before the movie started or hitting all the green lights on a busy urban stretch, little victories can bring an extra dose of joy to your drive. What small wins have had a big impact on your road trip?

- ☐ The gas pump stopped at a round number
- ☐ We crossed off everything on our itinerary
- ☐ We got a complimentary hotel upgrade
- ☐ We got a complimentary rental car upgrade
- ☐ Our favorite song came on the radio
- ☐ We found the perfect parking space
- ☐ Our favorite movie was playing on the hotel TV
- ☐ We got an early check-in
- ☐ We got a late checkout
- ☐ We hit smooth traffic all day
- ☐ There were clear skies the whole trip
- ☐ We drove into a sunset
- ☐ We were the only ones at a big attraction
- ☐ We stayed under budget
- ☐ We got free admission to an attraction
- ☐ ____________
- ☐ ____________
- ☐ ____________
- ☐ ____________

DATE:

THE FIVE SENSES

We often describe where we went on a road trip solely by what we saw, but there are so many more senses to explore. What did you hear? Smell? Feel? Taste? Take a moment at a few different locations to appreciate everything you're experiencing through all your senses. Record your observations here.

	What We...				
ATTRACTION	Saw	Heard	Smelled	Felt	Tasted

ROAD TRIP

STRETCH #:

DATE:

TO:

STARTING POINT:

ENDING POINT:

TODAY'S DRIVER(S):

WEATHER TODAY:

MUST-SEE STOPS

- ☐
- ☐
- ☐
- ☐
- ☐
- ☐

ITINERARY

MORNING:

AFTERNOON:

NIGHT:

What was our first impression of one of today's stops and how did it change by the time we left?

What were we most excited to see at one of today's stops and did it end up being our favorite part?

What is our least favorite part of travel? Why?

TRAVEL NOTES

ROAD TRIP "RULES"

DATE:

These road trip rules are meant to be fun. Have everyone in the car make up one random rule that must be obeyed throughout the entire course of the road trip. The rules can be anything you wish, such as "we cheer every time we see a Holiday Inn" or "if a mail truck passes us, we all high-five" or "we must take a car selfie whenever we enter a new state." The sillier the rule is, the more fun you'll have!

RULE ONE

RULE TWO

RULE THREE

RULE FOUR

RULE FIVE

DATE:

FORTUNATELY/UNFORTUNATELY

All road trips have their ups and downs. Tell a story that celebrates those bumps in the road. In this game, you will tell a story where each sentence alternates between starting with "fortunately" or "unfortunately." For example: "Jake was taking a road trip. Unfortunately, he forgot to pack toiletries. Fortunately, the hotel had free shampoo. Unfortunately, they were out of toothpaste." Everyone can tell their own complete story, or you can take turns with each passenger saying one sentence and see where the misadventure goes.

Write your favorite fortunately/unfortunately story here.

ROAD TRIP

STRETCH #:

DATE:

TO:

STARTING POINT:

ENDING POINT:

TODAY'S DRIVER(S):

WEATHER TODAY:

MUST-SEE STOPS

- ☐
- ☐
- ☐
- ☐
- ☐
- ☐

ITINERARY

MORNING:

AFTERNOON:

NIGHT:

What was our first impression of one of today's stops and how did it change by the time we left?

What were we most excited to see at one of today's stops and did it end up being our favorite part?

What is the best travel advice we've ever received?

TRAVEL NOTES

DATE:

TEN THINGS IN COMMON

You probably have lots of things in common with your road trip companions. For one thing, you're all traveling to the same place! Beyond that, what else brings you together? Do you all go to the same school? Bond over knitting or hockey? Battle for high scores in the same video games? Try to come up with at least ten things you all share, and if that number is too easy, keep it going!

1. ____________________

2. ____________________

3. ____________________

4. ____________________

5. ____________________

6. ____________________

7. ____________________

8. ____________________

9. ____________________

10. ____________________

FIRST WORD YOU SEE

DATE:

At a fork in the road and want to know what lies ahead? Let this puzzle steer you in the right direction. The first three words you see are what you can expect to experience on this road trip.

A	R	G	S	L	O	V	E	S	C	D	D	R	E	S	T	H	P
N	E	C	W	N	O	S	T	A	L	G	I	A	O	I	Y	A	V
T	J	V	P	K	S	E	R	E	N	I	T	Y	F	O	G	P	K
I	U	F	R	I	E	N	D	S	H	I	P	A	U	G	M	P	V
C	V	A	W	E	O	I	C	I	C	A	L	M	N	Y	A	I	J
I	E	T	J	O	Y	R	V	T	A	E	X	J	Z	U	G	N	V
P	N	E	X	C	I	T	E	M	E	N	T	L	N	R	I	E	W
A	A	M	Y	F	U	L	F	I	L	L	M	E	N	T	C	S	F
T	T	X	X	L	A	U	G	H	T	E	R	S	X	F	Q	S	P
I	I	C	P	V	N	F	R	E	E	D	O	M	G	L	J	B	F
O	O	M	W	O	N	D	E	R	S	P	E	A	C	E	R	F	N
N	N	A	D	V	E	N	T	U	R	E	R	Z	U	R	I	H	O

Name:

Words:

Name:

Words:

Name:

Words:

Name:

Words:

Words in puzzle: magic, adventure, happiness, peace, freedom, excitement, joy, fun, nostalgia, rejuvenation, anticipation, awe, wonder, serenity, fulfillment, love, laughter, friendship, calm, rest

ROAD TRIP

STRETCH #:

DATE:

TO:

STARTING POINT:

ENDING POINT:

TODAY'S DRIVER(S):

WEATHER TODAY:

MUST-SEE STOPS

☐

☐

☐

☐

☐

☐

ITINERARY

MORNING:

AFTERNOON:

NIGHT:

What was our first impression of one of today's stops and how did it change by the time we left?

What were we most excited to see at one of today's stops and did it end up being our favorite part?

What is the strongest emotion we've felt on this trip?

TRAVEL NOTES

Keep your eyes on the road while still playing a game with this road trip scavenger hunt. If you look hard enough, you'll be certain to find all of these things on your drive. Each item can also make a fun stop or a silly selfie, so have your camera phones ready and see how long it takes you to find them all.

ROAD TRIP SCAVENGER HUNT

DATE:

- ☐ A "Welcome to..." state sign
- ☐ A souvenir with your name on it
- ☐ A world's largest roadside attraction
- ☐ A funny license plate
- ☐ A scenic view
- ☐ Your dream car
- ☐ An awesome mural
- ☐ A detour sign
- ☐ A diner coffee mug
- ☐ A dog in a car
- ☐ A roadside fruit/vegetable stand
- ☐ A fun museum
- ☐ A town with a weird name
- ☐ A neon motel sign
- ☐ A building with interesting architecture
- ☐ An RV
- ☐ ______________________
- ☐ ______________________
- ☐ ______________________

DATE:

GREEN LIGHT, RED LIGHT, YELLOW LIGHT

Decompress after a long day in the car by reflecting on your adventures and what's to come by sharing a green, red, and yellow light moment.

- **Green Light:** Share something good about the day. It could be your favorite stop, stretch of drive, meal, or moment.
- **Red Light:** Share something that was a challenge. Maybe you didn't eat lunch until way later than expected, or maybe a traffic jam set your itinerary behind.
- **Yellow Light:** Share something you are looking forward to for the next day.

Name:

Green Light:

Red Light:

Yellow Light:

Name:

Green Light:

Red Light:

Yellow Light:

Name:

Green Light:

Red Light:

Yellow Light:

Name:

Green Light:

Red Light:

Yellow Light:

ROAD TRIP

STRETCH #: DATE:

TO:

STARTING POINT: ENDING POINT:

TODAY'S DRIVER(S):

WEATHER TODAY:

MUST-SEE STOPS

☐

☐

☐

☐

☐

☐

ITINERARY

MORNING:

AFTERNOON:

NIGHT:

What was our first impression of one of today's stops and how did it change by the time we left?

What were we most excited to see at one of today's stops and did it end up being our favorite part?

What souvenirs are we collecting? Why?

TRAVEL NOTES

SOUVENIR SHOP CHALLENGE

DATE:

Souvenir options abound when you're on the road—pull over at any local attraction or truck stop and you'll find rows of shelves filled with everything from handcrafted baskets to plastic bobbleheads. Before your road trip, pick something to collect along the way and look for at every stop. Or make it a game! Pick a souvenir type you all have to shop for on your trip. It could be postcards printed with puns, mini sheriff badges personalized with your names, or risqué floaty pens.

Try to outdo each other by finding the cheesiest mementos you can. Here are the most common souvenirs you'll find to give you ideas:

- Magnets
- Snow globes
- Hats
- Pins
- Pressed pennies
- Keychains
- Bumper stickers
- T-shirts
- Stickers
- Ornaments
- Postcards
- Shot glasses

WHAT IS THE BEST SOUVENIR YOU FOUND?

Name: ____________________

Souvenir: ____________________

Name: ____________________

Souvenir: ____________________

Name: ____________________

Souvenir: ____________________

Name: ____________________

Souvenir: ____________________

DATE:

EXPRESS LANE

Pick a topic, any topic! Choose dog breeds, rom-coms, latte flavors, or anything else you think you can name a lot of in a short period of time. Set a timer for three minutes and enter the Express Lane: Start listing things that fit your chosen topic until you've exhausted all of your ideas. Whoever ends up with the most answers wins. Use the ideas listed here to get started or come up with your own.

- ☐ Fast Food Items
- ☐ Ice Cream Flavors
- ☐ US Cities
- ☐ Reality TV Show Titles
- ☐ Broadway Musicals
- ☐ National Parks
- ☐ Sports Teams
- ☐ Zoo Animals
- ☐ Fruits
- ☐ Items of Clothing

- ☐ ____________
- ☐ ____________
- ☐ ____________
- ☐ ____________
- ☐ ____________
- ☐ ____________
- ☐ ____________

Winner: ____________

Number of Items: ____________

Runner-up: ____________

Number of Items: ____________

ROAD TRIP

STRETCH #:

DATE:

TO:

STARTING POINT:

ENDING POINT:

TODAY'S DRIVER(S):

WEATHER TODAY:

MUST-SEE STOPS

- [ ]
- [ ]
- [ ]
- [ ]
- [ ]
- [ ]

ITINERARY

MORNING:

AFTERNOON:

NIGHT:

What was our first impression of one of today's stops and how did it change by the time we left?

What were we most excited to see at one of today's stops and did it end up being our favorite part?

If we could have three wishes granted for this trip, what would they be?

TRAVEL NOTES

NAME THAT SONG

DATE:

Make a game out of picking fun driving tunes while trying to stump your friends to see if they can guess the title and/or artist. Take turns playing the first few notes from a song in your music library to see if anyone can guess what song it is. No correct guesses? Keep playing the song until someone can name the song and artist. Dig deep into your music library to find an oft-forgotten ballad or an oldie but goodie. Get creative—choose songs related to your destination or the theme of your trip! Jot down the winners here to see who among you has the best ear.

Guesser: ______________________________

Song: ______________ Artist: ______________

Guesser: ______________________________

Song: ______________ Artist: ______________

Guesser: ______________________________

Song: ______________ Artist: ______________

Guesser: ______________________________

Song: ______________ Artist: ______________

Guesser: ______________________________

Song: ______________ Artist: ______________

Guesser: ______________________________

Song: ______________ Artist: ______________

SHOW AND TELL

DATE:

What's the coolest thing you packed in your luggage? Are you just waiting for someone to ask you about it? Travel back to your childhood and play a game of show and tell in your car. Pick out something awesome that you packed or bought along the way. Show off the melted snowman snow globe souvenir you picked up in Tampa, the perfect pair of cowboy boots you'll be wearing to the State Fair of Texas, or the new solar-powered headlamp you brought for your night hike. Tell everyone what you brought and why you think they just have to see it. Take turns assessing everyone's item and fill in the stars to show the group's average rating.

Name:

Item:

Rating: ☆ ☆ ☆ ☆ ☆

Name:

Item:

Rating: ☆ ☆ ☆ ☆ ☆

Name:

Item:

Rating: ☆ ☆ ☆ ☆ ☆

Name:

Item:

Rating: ☆ ☆ ☆ ☆ ☆

Name:

Item:

Rating: ☆ ☆ ☆ ☆ ☆

Name:

Item:

Rating: ☆ ☆ ☆ ☆ ☆

Name:

Item:

Rating: ☆ ☆ ☆ ☆ ☆

Name:

Item:

Rating: ☆ ☆ ☆ ☆ ☆

ROAD TRIP

STRETCH #:

DATE:

TO:

STARTING POINT:

ENDING POINT:

TODAY'S DRIVER(S):

WEATHER TODAY:

MUST-SEE STOPS

- [ ]
- [ ]
- [ ]
- [ ]
- [ ]
- [ ]

ITINERARY

MORNING:

AFTERNOON:

NIGHT:

What was our first impression of one of today's stops and how did it change by the time we left?

What were we most excited to see at one of today's stops and did it end up being our favorite part?

What was a difficult part of this trip and how did we get through it?

TRAVEL NOTES

HYPOTHETICALS

Hypothetically, a lot of things can go wrong on a road trip. Take some time to ponder what you and your group would do in different hypothetical situations that we all hope we never have to encounter on the road.

DATE:

What would we do if we ran out of gas in the middle of nowhere?

What would we do if we had to survive in the wilderness for a night?

What would we do if we lost all our luggage?

What would we do if we witnessed a UFO landing?

What would we do if we were stuck behind a herd of bison?

What would we do if we got locked in a museum?

What would we do if we found Bigfoot?

DATE:

ROAD TRIP STOPS

Where does your group like to stop along the road to break up the trip? While one person might love spending some time in the great outdoors, others might prefer the comfort of an air-conditioned art museum. What are your group's favorite places to stop at on a road trip? Check them off the following list, then add your own favorites.

- ☐ Amusement parks
- ☐ Antique shops
- ☐ Ballparks
- ☐ Beaches
- ☐ Breweries
- ☐ Campsites
- ☐ Cemeteries
- ☐ Cities
- ☐ Curio shops
- ☐ Diners
- ☐ Drive-throughs
- ☐ Gas stations
- ☐ Geocaches
- ☐ Haunted sites
- ☐ Hiking trails
- ☐ Historical sites
- ☐ Hotels
- ☐ Motels
- ☐ Murals
- ☐ Museums
- ☐ National monuments
- ☐ National parks
- ☐ Natural wonders
- ☐ Nature preserves
- ☐ Neon signs
- ☐ Produce stands
- ☐ Rest areas
- ☐ Roadside attractions
- ☐ RV parks
- ☐ Scenic overlooks
- ☐ Small towns
- ☐ State fairs
- ☐ State signs
- ☐ Waterfalls
- ☐ Wineries
- ☐ ....
- ☐ ....
- ☐ ....
- ☐ ....

ROAD TRIP

STRETCH #:

DATE:

TO:

STARTING POINT:

ENDING POINT:

TODAY'S DRIVER(S):

WEATHER TODAY:

MUST-SEE STOPS

- [ ]
- [ ]
- [ ]
- [ ]
- [ ]
- [ ]

ITINERARY

MORNING:

AFTERNOON:

NIGHT:

What was our first impression of one of today's stops and how did it change by the time we left?

What were we most excited to see at one of today's stops and did it end up being our favorite part?

If we were to do anything differently on our next trip, what would it be?

TRAVEL NOTES

ROAD TRIP RITUALS

DATE:

Many travelers have road trip rituals—traditions that they always carry out on road trips. It could be stopping at that one particular diner for sandwiches and coffee, staying at the same hotel chain every night, collecting shot glasses from every state, or pulling over for freshly picked fruit when they see a roadside stand. What road trip rituals does your group have? What traditions do you want to start? It could be something you will do on every day of this trip or something you promise to do on every trip to come. Use the following ideas to get started, then come up with your own unique plans.

- ☐ Take a photo in the same pose everywhere you go.
- ☐ Watch a movie featuring the destination on the first night.
- ☐ Print photo albums after your trip.
- ☐ Start each day with a car selfie.
- ☐ Pick one chain to stop at every time you need gas.
- ☐ End each night with a refreshing drink by the hotel pool.

OUR ROAD TRIP RITUALS

- ☐ ______________________________
- ☐ ______________________________
- ☐ ______________________________
- ☐ ______________________________
- ☐ ______________________________
- ☐ ______________________________
- ☐ ______________________________

DATE:

ROAD TRIP

DARES

I dare you to not have fun playing this road trip game! Take turns challenging each other to road-friendly dares. Only the sunroof is the limit when posing a challenge: Just make sure they are car- (or destination-) friendly and safe for everyone involved. Use the prompts listed here or fill in some creative dares of your own.

I DARE YOU TO...

- ☐ Ask a stranger for directions.
- ☐ Blast classical music on the car radio.
- ☐ Dance in front of an attraction.
- ☐ Order the weirdest thing on the menu.
- ☐ Show what is in your toiletry bag.
- ☐ Send a postcard to a random address.
- ☐ Knock on a random hotel door and yell "Room service!"
- ☐ Eat a gas station hot dog.
- ☐ Switch clothes with another passenger.

- ☐ ....
- ☐ ....
- ☐ ....
- ☐ ....
- ☐ ....
- ☐ ....

ROAD TRIP

STRETCH #:

DATE:

TO:

STARTING POINT:

ENDING POINT:

TODAY'S DRIVER(S):

WEATHER TODAY:

MUST-SEE STOPS

- [ ]
- [ ]
- [ ]
- [ ]
- [ ]
- [ ]

ITINERARY

MORNING:

AFTERNOON:

NIGHT:

What was our first impression of one of today's stops and how did it change by the time we left?

What were we most excited to see at one of today's stops and did it end up being our favorite part?

What did we do on this stretch that was most outside of our comfort zones?

TRAVEL NOTES

DATE:

THE FORBIDDEN WORD

As you begin your road trip, choose a word among yourselves: a forbidden word. It should be something that is fairly common: something you're likely to say, but not so usual you'd be saying it in every other sentence (think "U-turn" and not "you"). Anytime someone says this forbidden word, tally up one point for them. At the end of the trip, the person with the least number of points wins.

Word: ______________________

Player: ______________ Points: ______

Player: ______________ Points: ______

Player: ______________ Points: ______

Player: ______________ Points: ______

Word: ______________________

Player: ______________ Points: ______

Player: ______________ Points: ______

Player: ______________ Points: ______

Player: ______________ Points: ______

BACKSEAT BLUNDERS

DATE:

No one is perfect—everyone has their faults and will make a mistake every once in a while. Which of these road trip faux pas are you guilty of? Add a point every time someone does something on the list. The winner is the one who has the fewest points at the end of the trip.

	NAME:	NAME:	NAME:	NAME:
Needs an extra rest stop	☐	☐	☐	☐
Says "Are we there yet?"	☐	☐	☐	☐
Skips a good song	☐	☐	☐	☐
Falls asleep in the car	☐	☐	☐	☐
Makes a wrong turn	☐	☐	☐	☐
Misses an exit ramp	☐	☐	☐	☐
Forgets to book ahead	☐	☐	☐	☐
Spills food in the car	☐	☐	☐	☐
Runs out of gas	☐	☐	☐	☐
Runs out of money	☐	☐	☐	☐
Sleeps in	☐	☐	☐	☐
Plans too much in a day	☐	☐	☐	☐
Plans too little in a day	☐	☐	☐	☐
Loses the car keys	☐	☐	☐	☐

Name: ______________________ Points: ________

Name: ______________________ Points: ________

Name: ______________________ Points: ________

Name: ______________________ Points: ________

ROAD TRIP

STRETCH #:

DATE:

TO:

STARTING POINT:

ENDING POINT:

TODAY'S DRIVER(S):

WEATHER TODAY:

MUST-SEE STOPS

- [ ]
- [ ]
- [ ]
- [ ]
- [ ]
- [ ]

ITINERARY

MORNING:

AFTERNOON:

NIGHT:

What was our first impression of one of today's stops and how did it change by the time we left?

What were we most excited to see at one of today's stops and did it end up being our favorite part?

What do we know now that we wish we had known at the beginning of our trip?

TRAVEL NOTES

DATE:

WHO WOULD WIN?

If the characters from *Stranger Things* went on a camping trip, Nancy might have the full itinerary mapped out, while Will would be running from the woods. And when it comes to Marvel, Black Widow can navigate with the best of them, but Hulk might lose his temper one too many times. Pit fictional character against fictional character to decide once and for all who would make the perfect road trip passenger. Take turns choosing a prompt and suggesting two characters from your favorite movies, books, or TV shows, then have a friendly debate among yourselves. Circle who you think ultimately comes out on top.

Who would be the better driver?

Character One: __________ vs Character Two: __________

Who would get lost the most?

Character One: __________ vs Character Two: __________

Who would plan the best route?

Character One: __________ vs Character Two: __________

Who would be better at roughing it?

Character One: __________ vs Character Two: __________

Who would finish the hike first?

Character One: __________ vs Character Two: __________

Who would find the best hotel deals?

Character One: __________ vs Character Two: __________

WE'RE TAKING A ROAD TRIP...

You're taking a road trip, and you want your friends to come with you, but whether they are allowed in the car or not depends on what they packed. In this guessing game, a "driver" asks everyone else in the car to take turns declaring what they packed for a road trip. It could be a shampoo bottle, playing cards, a beach towel, sunglasses, a camera, or anything else you might tuck into your suitcase. But the driver has made up a secret rule. It could be that the items have to begin with the same letter as their name (or any particular letter). It could be that it has to be something used while camping. The rule can be anything the driver wants. Passengers take turns declaring items and the driver either accepts or rejects them based on the secret rule. Passengers continue declaring items until someone can guess the secret rule that connects them all.

DATE:

Driver 1: ....

Rule: ....

Driver 2: ....

Rule: ....

Driver 3: ....

Rule: ....

Driver 4: ....

Rule: ....

ROAD TRIP

STRETCH #:

DATE:

TO:

STARTING POINT:

ENDING POINT:

TODAY'S DRIVER(S):

WEATHER TODAY:

MUST-SEE STOPS

- [ ]
- [ ]
- [ ]
- [ ]
- [ ]
- [ ]

ITINERARY

MORNING:

AFTERNOON:

NIGHT:

What was our first impression of one of today's stops and how did it change by the time we left?

What were we most excited to see at one of today's stops and did it end up being our favorite part?

What would our perfect day on vacation look like?

TRAVEL NOTES

WHICH OF THESE ROADSIDE ATTRACTIONS HAVE YOU SEEN?

DATE:

Roadside attractions are peculiar sites designed to lure travelers off the highway. They come in many different shapes, sizes, materials, and functions, but some of the most popular are oversized versions of everyday things. After all, the larger the object, the easier it is to spot from a car. How many of these oddities have you seen on your travels? Put initials after each of these iconic roadside attractions that each person has visited. Tally them up to find out who has seen the most!

World's Largest Office Chair (Alabama)
Igloo City (Alaska)
The Thing (Arizona)
Monster Mart (Arkansas)
Cabazon Dinosaurs (California)
UFO Watchtower (Colorado)
PEZ Visitor Center (Connecticut)
Miles the Monster (Delaware)
Swampy: World's Largest Alligator (Florida)
The Big Chicken (Georgia)
Elvis Aloha Statue (Hawaii)
Idaho Potato Museum (Idaho)
World's Largest Catsup Bottle (Illinois)
World's Largest Ball of Paint (Indiana)
Albert the Bull (Iowa)
World's Largest Ball of Twine (Kansas)
World's Largest Bat (Kentucky)
Abita Mystery House (Louisiana)
Eartha: World's Largest Rotating Globe (Maine)
Nipper, the RCA Dog (Maryland)
Hood Milk Bottle (Massachusetts)
World's Largest Cherry Pie (Michigan)
Paul Bunyan and *Babe the Blue Ox* (Minnesota)
Margaret's Grocery (Mississippi)
World's Second-Largest Fork (Missouri)
Penguin Colossus (Montana)
Carhenge (Nebraska)
Alien Research Center (Nevada)
Redstone Rocket (New Hampshire)
Lucy the Elephant (New Jersey)
World's Largest Pistachio (New Mexico)
The Big Duck (New York)
World's Largest Chest of Drawers (North Carolina)
Salem Sue: World's Largest Holstein Cow (North Dakota)
World's Largest Basket (Ohio)
Blue Whale of Catoosa (Oklahoma)
Harvey the Giant Rabbit (Oregon)
Haines Shoe House (Pennsylvania)
Big Blue Bug (Rhode Island)
South of the Border (South Carolina)
Wall Drug (South Dakota)
Airplane Service Station (Tennessee)
Cadillac Ranch (Texas)
Hole N" the Rock (Utah)
World's Tallest Filing Cabinet (Vermont)
Foamhenge (Virginia)
The *Fremont Troll* (Washington)
Mothman Statue (West Virginia)
House on the Rock (Wisconsin)
World's Largest Jackalope (Wyoming)
Mac the Moose (Saskatchewan)
World's Largest Dinosaur (Alberta)
World's Largest Hockey Stick and Puck (British Columbia)
Giant Toonie (Ontario)
World's Largest Axe (New Brunswick)
World's Largest Fiddle (Nova Scotia)
Gibeau Orange Julep (Quebec)

DATE:

GREETINGS FROM...

When it comes to picking out postcards, do you go for beautiful scenery, a local landmark, or a funny (or slightly inappropriate) joke? Use the space on this page to design a picture-perfect postcard worth writing home about.

ROAD TRIP

STRETCH #: DATE:

TO:

STARTING POINT: ENDING POINT:

TODAY'S DRIVER(S):

WEATHER TODAY:

MUST-SEE STOPS

- [ ]
- [ ]
- [ ]
- [ ]
- [ ]
- [ ]

ITINERARY

MORNING:

AFTERNOON:

NIGHT:

What was our first impression of one of today's stops and how did it change by the time we left?

What were we most excited to see at one of today's stops and did it end up being our favorite part?

What is the funniest thing that happened on this road trip?

TRAVEL NOTES

CAR QUOTES

"Are we there yet?" might be the most common quote associated with road trips. But you can do better than that! Use this page to record the most memorable things you or your travel companions said on your journey.

DATE:

" ____________________ "

Said by: ____________________

" ____________________ "

Said by: ____________________

" ____________________ "

Said by: ____________________

" ____________________ "

Said by: ____________________

" ____________________ "

Said by: ____________________

" ____________________ "

Said by: ____________________

" ____________________ "

Said by: ____________________

DATE:

TRAVELING TALENT SHOW

What's the most impressive talent you have that can be performed within the small confines of a car? Whether it's a comedy routine, mind reading, or tying a cherry stem with your tongue, show off the skills your friends didn't even know you had in a traveling talent show. Take turns flaunting your abilities, then rate everyone's talent here. (Hint: You all deserve five stars!)

Name:

Talent:

Rating: ☆ ☆ ☆ ☆ ☆

Name:

Talent:

Rating: ☆ ☆ ☆ ☆ ☆

Name:

Talent:

Rating: ☆ ☆ ☆ ☆ ☆

Name:

Talent:

Rating: ☆ ☆ ☆ ☆ ☆

Name:

Talent:

Rating: ☆ ☆ ☆ ☆ ☆

Name:

Talent:

Rating: ☆ ☆ ☆ ☆ ☆

Name:

Talent:

Rating: ☆ ☆ ☆ ☆ ☆

Name:

Talent:

Rating: ☆ ☆ ☆ ☆ ☆

Name:

Talent:

Rating: ☆ ☆ ☆ ☆ ☆

Name:

Talent:

Rating: ☆ ☆ ☆ ☆ ☆

ROAD TRIP

STRETCH #:

DATE:

TO:

STARTING POINT:

ENDING POINT:

TODAY'S DRIVER(S):

WEATHER TODAY:

MUST-SEE STOPS

- ☐
- ☐
- ☐
- ☐
- ☐
- ☐

ITINERARY

MORNING:

AFTERNOON:

NIGHT:

What was our first impression of one of today's stops and how did it change by the time we left?

What were we most excited to see at one of today's stops and did it end up being our favorite part?

What is something we brought with us that we will always pack in the future?

TRAVEL NOTES

OUT OF OFFICE

Road trips are for play, not work. So hopefully you set up that out-of-office message and left your laptop at home. In this activity, challenge each other to see who can come up with the most entertaining out-of-office message. No boring "I'll respond when I'm back in the office on Monday" allowed here. (Bonus bragging rights if you actually put it to use!)

DATE:

Name:

Out-of-Office Message:

Name:

Out-of-Office Message:

Name:

Out-of-Office Message:

Name:

Out-of-Office Message:

UNPOPULAR OPINIONS

DATE:

How close are you with your fellow road trippers? Sometimes it's what a group doesn't like that brings them closer together. Are your unpopular opinions the same?

Overrated Movie

Name: ______ Answer: ______

Name: ______ Answer: ______

Name: ______ Answer: ______

Name: ______ Answer: ______

Trend You Can't Stand

Name: ______ Answer: ______

Name: ______ Answer: ______

Name: ______ Answer: ______

Name: ______ Answer: ______

Worst TV Show

Name: ______ Answer: ______

Name: ______ Answer: ______

Name: ______ Answer: ______

Name: ______ Answer: ______

Least Favorite Social Media Channel

Name: ______ Answer: ______

Name: ______ Answer: ______

Name: ______ Answer: ______

Name: ______ Answer: ______

ROAD TRIP

STRETCH #:

DATE:

TO:

STARTING POINT:

ENDING POINT:

TODAY'S DRIVER(S):

WEATHER TODAY:

MUST-SEE STOPS

☐

☐

☐

☐

☐

☐

ITINERARY

MORNING:

AFTERNOON:

NIGHT:

What was our first impression of one of today's stops and how did it change by the time we left?

What were we most excited to see at one of today's stops and did it end up being our favorite part?

What would we add to our itinerary if money was no object?

TRAVEL NOTES

GUESS WHERE

DATE:

Pick a travel destination: It can be anything from Denver to Thailand to White Sands National Park to the World's Largest Holstein Cow. Have everyone else in the car try to guess where in the world you chose. Each passenger gets to ask ten yes or no questions to try to figure out your destination. If the player keeps their locale of choice a secret, they win!

After the location is revealed, write it down here along with whose idea it was, who guessed it, and what gave it away.

Player: ________ Location: ________

Guesser: ________ What gave it away? ________

Player: ________ Location: ________

Guesser: ________ What gave it away? ________

Player: ________ Location: ________

Guesser: ________ What gave it away? ________

Player: ________ Location: ________

Guesser: ________ What gave it away? ________

Player: ________ Location: ________

Guesser: ________ What gave it away? ________

Player: ________ Location: ________

Guesser: ________ What gave it away? ________

DATE:

TAKE A RANDOM ROUTE

Explore a new-to-you town by taking a turn at chance. Before you enter the town, circle "left," "right," or "straight" in each numbered row. Then, every time you reach a stop sign or stoplight, follow the list down, turning right, left, or going straight, depending on which one you circled. Once you've completed your last move, see where you ended up and what you find.

CIRCLE A DIRECTION

1. LEFT RIGHT STRAIGHT
2. LEFT RIGHT STRAIGHT
3. LEFT RIGHT STRAIGHT
4. LEFT RIGHT STRAIGHT
5. LEFT RIGHT STRAIGHT
6. LEFT RIGHT STRAIGHT
7. LEFT RIGHT STRAIGHT
8. LEFT RIGHT STRAIGHT
9. LEFT RIGHT STRAIGHT
10. LEFT RIGHT STRAIGHT
11. LEFT RIGHT STRAIGHT
12. LEFT RIGHT STRAIGHT
13. LEFT RIGHT STRAIGHT
14. LEFT RIGHT STRAIGHT
15. LEFT RIGHT STRAIGHT
16. LEFT RIGHT STRAIGHT
17. LEFT RIGHT STRAIGHT
18. LEFT RIGHT STRAIGHT
19. LEFT RIGHT STRAIGHT
20. LEFT RIGHT STRAIGHT

WHERE DID YOU END UP?

ROAD TRIP

STRETCH #:

DATE:

TO:

STARTING POINT:

ENDING POINT:

TODAY'S DRIVER(S):

WEATHER TODAY:

MUST-SEE STOPS

- [ ]
- [ ]
- [ ]
- [ ]
- [ ]
- [ ]

ITINERARY

MORNING:

AFTERNOON:

NIGHT:

What was our first impression of one of today's stops and how did it change by the time we left?

What were we most excited to see at one of today's stops and did it end up being our favorite part?

Which new words/local lingo did we pick up on our travels?

TRAVEL NOTES

GREAT MINDS

After long days in the car together, it's natural for everyone to start thinking alike. So put your mind meld to the test with a game of Great Minds. Pick a category and have everyone think of three things that fit. You get points based on how many people thought of the same answer as you. For example, if the category is "State that starts with the letter A" and three people say "Alabama," all of them get three points. Whoever has the most points at the end wins.

DATE:

CATEGORIES

- ☐ State that starts with the letter M
- ☐ Song with a person's name in the title
- ☐ Hotel chain
- ☐ Car maker
- ☐ Pizza topping
- ☐ Something you bring camping
- ☐ Something you find in a hotel room
- ☐ Drive-through foods
- ☐ ______________________________
- ☐ ______________________________

SCORING

Name: ______________________ Points: ________

Name: ______________________ Points: ________

Name: ______________________ Points: ________

Name: ______________________ Points: ________

RADIO ORACLE

Have a burning question on your mind and need a sign from the universe to answer it? Let your car radio serve as your divine seer. Take turns asking questions that you need a little clarification on. "Is my partner staying faithful back home?" "Should I quit my job and travel forever?" "Where should I road trip to next?" Scan the radio to the next station (or shuffle a playlist to the next song) and let the lyrics to whatever song comes up answer your query. Write down what you learn here.

DATE:

Player: ________ Question: ________

Song: ________

Answer: ________

Player: ________ Question: ________

Song: ________

Answer: ________

Player: ________ Question: ________

Song: ________

Answer: ________

Player: ________ Question: ________

Song: ________

Answer: ________

ROAD TRIP

STRETCH #:

DATE:

TO:

STARTING POINT:

ENDING POINT:

TODAY'S DRIVER(S):

WEATHER TODAY:

MUST-SEE STOPS

- ☐
- ☐
- ☐
- ☐
- ☐
- ☐

ITINERARY

MORNING:

AFTERNOON:

NIGHT:

What was our first impression of one of today's stops and how did it change by the time we left?

What were we most excited to see at one of today's stops and did it end up being our favorite part?

What local retail chain did we visit that we wish we had at home?

TRAVEL NOTES

NEW CHAIN VISIT

DATE:

You've probably seen your fair share of Burger Kings or BPs on the road. But have you ever encountered a Buc-ee's, Wawa, Tim Hortons, or Cook Out? No matter where you travel, you'll likely run across a regionally popular restaurant or gas station chain that you don't have back home. Keep an eye out for road signs and billboards for new-to-you chains. And if you've never eaten at Skyline Chili or seen a Sinclair dinosaur up close, pull over and try one of those instead of your usual go-tos. Write down which regional chains you found and what everyone thought of them.

Chain: ____________ Category: ____________

State: ____ What did you eat or see? ____________

What do you think?

____

Chain: ____________ Category: ____________

State: ____ What did you eat or see? ____________

What do you think?

____

Chain: ____________ Category: ____________

State: ____ What did you eat or see? ____________

What do you think?

____

Who on your road trip is most responsible for taking the wheel and keeping everything moving forward? And who should probably be sent back to driver's ed? Read this list of idiosyncrasies out loud and have everyone point to the person who they think exemplifies each. Write down who the majority rules.

POLL THE PASSENGERS

DATE:

Who planned the most? ______

Who paid for the most? ______

Who was the most organized? ______

Who asks to stop the most? ______

Who wakes up earliest? ______

Who takes the longest time to get ready? ______

Who packed the most? ______

Who takes the most photos? ______

Who has the best taste in driving music? ______

Who is the best driver? ______

Who complains the most? ______

Who sleeps in the car the most? ______

Who is the most adventurous? ______

ROAD TRIP

STRETCH #:

DATE:

TO:

STARTING POINT:

ENDING POINT:

TODAY'S DRIVER(S):

WEATHER TODAY:

MUST-SEE STOPS

- [ ]
- [ ]
- [ ]
- [ ]
- [ ]
- [ ]

ITINERARY

MORNING:

AFTERNOON:

NIGHT:

What was our first impression of one of today's stops and how did it change by the time we left?

What were we most excited to see at one of today's stops and did it end up being our favorite part?

What made us smile most today? Why?

TRAVEL NOTES

THE COMPLIMENT GAME

Make your day in the car brighter by playing a sweet round of the Compliment Game. Go through the alphabet and use each letter to form a compliment for one of your friends. A is for Heather's adventurous attitude, B is for Shanna's beautiful belt, and so on. Make someone's day, from A to Z.

DATE:

A is for ______________

B is for ______________

C is for ______________

D is for ______________

E is for ______________

F is for ______________

G is for ______________

H is for ______________

I is for ______________

J is for ______________

K is for ______________

L is for ______________

M is for ______________

N is for ______________

O is for ______________

P is for ______________

Q is for ______________

R is for ______________

S is for ______________

T is for ______________

U is for ______________

V is for ______________

W is for ______________

X is for ______________

Y is for ______________

Z is for ______________

DATE:

MILKSHAKE WORD

At the start of your trip, have everyone choose their own "milkshake word." It can be any word you want, but it should be a term that isn't so obscure no one would ever say it but also not so common someone would say it all the time. Don't tell anyone what your word is, and write it down on a piece of paper, fold it, and tuck it away in a safe place. If, at any time during your road trip, someone unknowingly says your milkshake word out loud, stop the conversation by yelling out "Milkshake word!," pull over at the next convenient drive-through, and buy everyone in the car a round of milkshakes (or other special drink).

Name: ________ Word: ________ Was it said? **Yes** **No**

Who said it? ________ Where did you get milkshakes? ________

Name: ________ Word: ________ Was it said? **Yes** **No**

Who said it? ________ Where did you get milkshakes? ________

Name: ________ Word: ________ Was it said? **Yes** **No**

Who said it? ________ Where did you get milkshakes? ________

Name: ________ Word: ________ Was it said? **Yes** **No**

Who said it? ________ Where did you get milkshakes? ________

ROAD TRIP

STRETCH #:

DATE:

TO:

STARTING POINT:

ENDING POINT:

TODAY'S DRIVER(S):

WEATHER TODAY:

MUST-SEE STOPS

- [ ]
- [ ]
- [ ]
- [ ]
- [ ]
- [ ]

ITINERARY

MORNING:

AFTERNOON:

NIGHT:

What was our first impression of one of today's stops and how did it change by the time we left?

What were we most excited to see at one of today's stops and did it end up being our favorite part?

What is the most picturesque landscape we saw? What made it so picturesque?

TRAVEL NOTES

COLOR CONNECTION

Red cars, blue skies, black asphalt, green highway signs: You'll see so many colors every day of a road trip. It's easy to barely pay attention to them, though. For this activity, look for something that represents one of these hues and write about it here.

DATE:

RED	BLUE
ORANGE	BLACK
YELLOW	PINK
GREEN	WHITE

If you were to build your ultimate road trip, where would you go? What would you see? What would you drive? Answer those questions by generating your next road trip using the keys listed here.

ROAD TRIP GENERATOR

DATE:

__________ (name) is traveling to __________ to see a __________ and driving a __________.

__________ (name) is traveling to __________ to see a __________ and driving a __________.

__________ (name) is traveling to __________ to see a __________ and driving a __________.

__________ (name) is traveling to __________ to see a __________ and driving a __________.

Destination
First Letter of First Name:
A: Las Vegas, B: Portland, C: Denver, D: Miami, E: Savannah, F: New Orleans, G: Minneapolis, H: Charlotte, I: Seattle, J: New York City, K: Aspen, L: Toronto, M: Pittsburgh, N: Phoenix, O: Key West, P: Austin, Q: Milwaukee, R: San Francisco, S: Boston, T: Nashville, U: Santa Fe, V: Chicago, W: Vancouver, X: Omaha, Y: Cleveland, Z: Bar Harbor

Site
Birth Month:
January: World's Largest Cat
February: Pumpkin Farm
March: Dinosaur Theme Park
April: Space-Age Muffler Man
May: Haunted Bed and Breakfast
June: Natural Hot Spring
July: Alien Landing Point
August: Pink Sand Beach
September: Giant Narwhal
October: Banana Museum
November: Snowy Ski Resort
December: Mustard Factory

Transportation
Last Number of Your Phone Number: 0: Sedan, 1: Motorcycle, 2: Minivan, 3: Hatchback, 4: RV, 5: Convertible, 6: Campervan, 7: Station Wagon, 8: SUV, 9: Sports Car

ROAD TRIP

STRETCH #:

DATE:

TO:

STARTING POINT:

ENDING POINT:

TODAY'S DRIVER(S):

WEATHER TODAY:

MUST-SEE STOPS

- [ ]
- [ ]
- [ ]
- [ ]
- [ ]
- [ ]

ITINERARY

MORNING:

AFTERNOON:

NIGHT:

What was our first impression of one of today's stops and how did it change by the time we left?

What were we most excited to see at one of today's stops and did it end up being our favorite part?

What is a travel experience we're most grateful for?

TRAVEL NOTES

NAME THE STATES

DATE:

Can you name all fifty US states without cheating? Give it a go! Need a hint? Check out the License Plate Game on page 39 for a clue!

1. ________
2. ________
3. ________
4. ________
5. ________
6. ________
7. ________
8. ________
9. ________
10. ________
11. ________
12. ________
13. ________
14. ________
15. ________
16. ________
17. ________
18. ________
19. ________
20. ________
21. ________
22. ________
23. ________
24. ________
25. ________
26. ________
27. ________
28. ________
29. ________
30. ________
31. ________
32. ________
33. ________
34. ________
35. ________
36. ________
37. ________
38. ________
39. ________
40. ________
41. ________
42. ________
43. ________
44. ________
45. ________
46. ________
47. ________
48. ________
49. ________
50. ________

DATE:

PHOTO POSING CHALLENGE

One of the best ways to remember how much fun you had on your road trip is to take lots of group shots everywhere you go. But standing in a row and smiling at the camera can get a little stale. Mix it up by striking a different pose at every stop. Here's a list of group photo ideas to try. Check each one off and write down where and when you took the photo so you can find it in your camera roll.

	Where	When
☐ Facing backward		
☐ Hugging		
☐ Blow a kiss		
☐ Look confused		
☐ Over the shoulder		
☐ Extreme close-up		
☐ Funny faces		
☐ Charlie's Angels		
☐ Piggyback ride		
☐ Look away from the camera		
☐ Kissing		
☐ Looking at each other		

ROAD TRIP

STRETCH #:

DATE:

TO:

STARTING POINT:

ENDING POINT:

TODAY'S DRIVER(S):

WEATHER TODAY:

MUST-SEE STOPS

- [ ]
- [ ]
- [ ]
- [ ]
- [ ]
- [ ]

ITINERARY

MORNING:

AFTERNOON:

NIGHT:

What was our first impression of one of today's stops and how did it change by the time we left?

What were we most excited to see at one of today's stops and did it end up being our favorite part?

If we were to write a book about this trip, what would the title be and why?

TRAVEL NOTES

FAKE TOUR GUIDE

Take turns playing tour guide at different stops on your road trip. The fun part is that you don't have to actually know anything about where you are. Make up a history to a roadside attraction, facts about national park wildlife, or stories about your "haunted" hotel. See if you can trick your friends into believing some of your not-so-true facts. Or at least see if you can make them laugh with ridiculous trivia. Make up any fake facts you want, or use these fill-in-the-blank prompts to get your imagination going.

DATE:

This attraction was erected in ____________________.

It was built by ____________________.

It is made out of ____________________.

It was created because ____________________.

It is famous because ____________________.

It is secretly ____________________.

It is the color __________ because __________.

Legend has it ____________________

____________________.

It is haunted by ____________________.

Its most unique feature is ____________________

____________________.

____________________ people visit each year.

DATE:

DRAW A ROADSIDE ATTRACTION

Think big on this one! Stretch your imagination by thinking up a really amazing roadside attraction. Would it be the world's largest version of your favorite thing? A weird museum you could spend all day in? Or a bronze statue of your pet cat? Envision your ideal attraction and draw it in one of the spaces here. Share your idea with your friends and explain why you wish this dream roadside attraction was a reality, then invite them to draw their own.

ROAD TRIP

STRETCH #:

DATE:

TO:

STARTING POINT:

ENDING POINT:

TODAY'S DRIVER(S):

WEATHER TODAY:

MUST-SEE STOPS

- [ ]
- [ ]
- [ ]
- [ ]
- [ ]
- [ ]

ITINERARY

MORNING:

AFTERNOON:

NIGHT:

What was our first impression of one of today's stops and how did it change by the time we left?

What were we most excited to see at one of today's stops and did it end up being our favorite part?

What is something we've learned on this road trip?

TRAVEL NOTES

CAR BINGO

DATE:

Do you know your Hondas from your Toyotas? Decide on a list of vehicles to keep a lookout for on your trip. You can choose a specific make and model (Ford Bronco), color (orange), or type (electric). You can look for any automobile you want, from a motorcycle to a school bus to a clown car. Vehicles can only be claimed by the first person to spot them. So if one person claims that blue Jetta in front of you, everyone else has to wait until another one rolls along. The first person to spot all the vehicles on the list wins!

Car: ______________________

Spotter: ______________________

Car: ______________________

Spotter: ______________________

Car: ______________________

Spotter: ______________________

Car: ______________________

Spotter: ______________________

Car: ______________________

Spotter: ______________________

Car: ______________________

Spotter: ______________________

Car: ______________________

Spotter: ______________________

Car: ______________________

Spotter: ______________________

Car: ______________________

Spotter: ______________________

Car: ______________________

Spotter: ______________________

Car: ______________________

Spotter: ______________________

Car: ______________________

Spotter: ______________________

Car: ______________________

Spotter: ______________________

WINNER: ______________________

STATE SYMBOLS

DATE:

Every state has a list of official symbols, such as a state bird, animal, flower, vegetable, and motto. What do you think these are for the area you're driving through? Pay close attention to what you see in the state you're traveling in and take a guess at what the state symbols might be. Take it seriously or come up with some ridiculous answers. Look them up later to see how close you were!

STATE: ______

Bird: ______

Animal: ______

Flower: ______

Vegetable: ______

Motto: ______

STATE: ______

Bird: ______

Animal: ______

Flower: ______

Vegetable: ______

Motto: ______

STATE: ______

Bird: ______

Animal: ______

Flower: ______

Vegetable: ______

Motto: ______

STATE: ______

Bird: ______

Animal: ______

Flower: ______

Vegetable: ______

Motto: ______

ROAD TRIP

STRETCH #:

DATE:

TO:

STARTING POINT:

ENDING POINT:

TODAY'S DRIVER(S):

WEATHER TODAY:

MUST-SEE STOPS

☐

☐

☐

☐

☐

☐

ITINERARY

MORNING:

AFTERNOON:

NIGHT:

What was our first impression of one of today's stops and how did it change by the time we left?

What were we most excited to see at one of today's stops and did it end up being our favorite part?

What is something we did that we wish we could do every day?

TRAVEL NOTES

IMAGINE A CELEBRITY ROAD TRIP

DATE:

Road tripping with your own friends is definitely fun. But what if you were road tripping with the cast of *Friends*? Or *Bridgerton*? Or *Star Trek*? Choose a TV show, book, movie, or celebrity family, and build your road trip car. Who would be the best driver? Who do you want to sit shotgun and navigate? Who do you think is most likely to fall asleep in the back seat? And who would best be left locked away in the trunk? Decide where in the car you want every character to sit and why.

Category: ______________

Driving: ______________

Shotgun: ______________

Backseat Driver: ______________

Sleeping in the Back: ______________

Hiding in the Trunk: ______________

Category: ______________

Driving: ______________

Shotgun: ______________

Backseat Driver: ______________

Sleeping in the Back: ______________

Hiding in the Trunk: ______________

Category: ______________

Driving: ______________

Shotgun: ______________

Backseat Driver: ______________

Sleeping in the Back: ______________

Hiding in the Trunk: ______________

Category: ______________

Driving: ______________

Shotgun: ______________

Backseat Driver: ______________

Sleeping in the Back: ______________

Hiding in the Trunk: ______________

DATE:

SORRY I WAS LATE, BUT...

"Sorry I was late, but...I was touring a cloned dinosaur theme park and they all got loose." In this game, you'll each start a story with "Sorry I was late, but..." and then finish your tale with the plot from a movie. Your travel partners then have to guess what film you're describing. After all is revealed, write down the movie in question, who came up with the story, who guessed it, and what gave the answer away.

Player:

Guesser:

Movie:

What gave it away?

Player:

Guesser:

Movie:

What gave it away?

Player:

Guesser:

Movie:

What gave it away?

Player:

Guesser:

Movie:

What gave it away?

ROAD TRIP

STRETCH #:

DATE:

TO:

STARTING POINT:

ENDING POINT:

TODAY'S DRIVER(S):

WEATHER TODAY:

MUST-SEE STOPS

- [ ]
- [ ]
- [ ]
- [ ]
- [ ]
- [ ]

ITINERARY

MORNING:

AFTERNOON:

NIGHT:

What was our first impression of one of today's stops and how did it change by the time we left?

What were we most excited to see at one of today's stops and did it end up being our favorite part?

What's a travel experience that moved us to tears?

TRAVEL NOTES

PUT A FINGER DOWN:

ROAD TRIP EDITION

DATE:

Put a finger down if you love taking road trips! To play this game, put up both hands with all your fingers extended (if you're driving, just keep track mentally). Put a finger down for every one of these road trip milestones you've experienced. Whoever has put down the most fingers by the end wins. Ready to go? Put a finger down if you have…

1. Used a disgusting gas station bathroom.
2. Run out of gas.
3. Driven through the night to get somewhere.
4. Visited all fifty states.
5. Taken a solo road trip.
6. Gotten lost on a road trip.
7. Left something important at home.
8. Lost cell phone service when you needed it.
9. Gotten carsick.
10. Made an unexpected detour.
11. Had a hotel lose your reservation.
12. Gotten caught in bad weather.
13. Run out of cell phone battery.
14. Gotten a flat tire.
15. Had the best time on this road trip!

Name:

Fingers Down:

Name:

Fingers Down:

Name:

Fingers Down:

Name:

Fingers Down:

RATE THE BATHROOMS

DATE:

When you've got to go, you've got to go! On a road trip, you don't always have the luxury to choose where to stop for a bathroom. Luckily, with restaurants, gas stations, rest stops, and visitor centers, you'll hopefully always find one when you need one. Some of those options might prove to be better than others. And some places will even brag on their billboards that they have the best restrooms for miles. Rate some of the best and worst bathrooms you've found on the road.

Location:

Stop Type:

Rating: ☆ ☆ ☆ ☆ ☆

Notes:

Location:

Stop Type:

Rating: ☆ ☆ ☆ ☆ ☆

Notes:

Location:

Stop Type:

Rating: ☆ ☆ ☆ ☆ ☆

Notes:

Location:

Stop Type:

Rating: ☆ ☆ ☆ ☆ ☆

Notes:

Location:

Stop Type:

Rating: ☆ ☆ ☆ ☆ ☆

Notes:

Location:

Stop Type:

Rating: ☆ ☆ ☆ ☆ ☆

Notes:

ROAD TRIP

STRETCH #:

DATE:

TO:

STARTING POINT:

ENDING POINT:

TODAY'S DRIVER(S):

WEATHER TODAY:

MUST-SEE STOPS

- ☐
- ☐
- ☐
- ☐
- ☐
- ☐

ITINERARY

MORNING:

AFTERNOON:

NIGHT:

What was our first impression of one of today's stops and how did it change by the time we left?

What were we most excited to see at one of today's stops and did it end up being our favorite part?

Write down any traffic headaches we've encountered.

TRAVEL NOTES

TRAFFIC JAM-BOREE

DATE:

Stuck in traffic? Don't let a little gridlock get you down. Use it as an excuse to get to know your neighboring vehicles. Roll down all your windows and interact with those around you. Rack up points for various levels of reciprocal actions. Pit the right side of the car against the left to see who gets the most points.

1 POINT: WAVE

Wave at drivers and passengers on the road and pedestrians on the sidewalk. If someone waves back, you get one point.

2 POINTS: SING-ALONG

Open all your windows and blast a fun song: a hot new hit, an '80s throwback, or your favorite Broadway show tune. Sing along and see if you can get your neighboring cars to join in. For every car that joins your sing-along, your side gets two points.

3 POINTS: TAKING REQUESTS

Get a song request from another car and blast it for them to hear. Every request is worth three points.

POINT TOTALS

Right Side: ____________ Left Side: ____________ Winner: ____________________

What was the most memorable interaction?

____

____

WHICH NATIONAL PARKS

HAVE YOU VISITED?

DATE:

With opportunities for camping, hiking, climbing, and just taking in the momentous views, national parks make popular road trip pit stops and destinations. From Acadia to Zion, there are sixty-three national parks in the United States. Is your goal to visit them all? These are some of the most popular national parks; put a check mark after every one you've visited. Tally them up to see who has been to the most!

	NAME:	NAME:	NAME:	NAME:
Acadia National Park	☐	☐	☐	☐
Arches National Park	☐	☐	☐	☐
Bryce Canyon National Park	☐	☐	☐	☐
Capitol Reef National Park	☐	☐	☐	☐
Cuyahoga Valley National Park	☐	☐	☐	☐
Death Valley National Park	☐	☐	☐	☐
Glacier National Park	☐	☐	☐	☐
Grand Canyon National Park	☐	☐	☐	☐
Grand Teton National Park	☐	☐	☐	☐
Hot Springs National Park	☐	☐	☐	☐
Joshua Tree National Park	☐	☐	☐	☐
Mount Rainier National Park	☐	☐	☐	☐
Olympic National Park	☐	☐	☐	☐
Rocky Mountain National Park	☐	☐	☐	☐
Shenandoah National Park	☐	☐	☐	☐
Yellowstone National Park	☐	☐	☐	☐
Yosemite National Park	☐	☐	☐	☐
Zion National Park	☐	☐	☐	☐
Totals:				

ROAD TRIP

STRETCH #:

DATE:

TO:

STARTING POINT:

ENDING POINT:

TODAY'S DRIVER(S):

WEATHER TODAY:

MUST-SEE STOPS

- ☐
- ☐
- ☐
- ☐
- ☐
- ☐

ITINERARY

MORNING:

AFTERNOON:

NIGHT:

What was our first impression of one of today's stops and how did it change by the time we left?

What were we most excited to see at one of today's stops and did it end up being our favorite part?

Where on our route could we see ourselves living? Why?

TRAVEL NOTES

ATLAS

DATE:

Atlas is a fun way to pass time on a road trip while testing your knowledge of the world. Start with one person naming any country in the world. Then the next person names another country that starts with the last letter of the previous country. For example: Spain, Nigeria, Australia, and so on. Keep going until you can't think of one, and then start again! If geography is not your thing, you can also play this game with any other category you like, from musical artists to 1990s cartoons. Record your final results here to see how far through the alphabet you get!

GAME 1

Starting Word: ____________ Ending Word: ____________

GAME 2

Starting Word: ____________ Ending Word: ____________

GAME 3

Starting Word: ____________ Ending Word: ____________

GAME 4

Starting Word: ____________ Ending Word: ____________

GAME 5

Starting Word: ____________ Ending Word: ____________

GAME 6

Starting Word: ____________ Ending Word: ____________

HOTEL ROOM
SPOT THE DIFFERENCE

Check into your hotel room for the night, and then spend one minute walking around and getting a good look at the room. When the minute is up, have everyone stand in the hallway except one person. That person should then change five things in the room: hide a pillow in the closet, turn on a lamp, move a bottle of shampoo. The changes should be subtle but noticeable. When everyone returns, they have to trust their memory to figure out the differences. Record the changes here and check them off if they were discovered.

DATE:

Hotel: ____________

1. ____________
2. ____________
3. ____________
4. ____________
5. ____________

Hotel: ____________

1. ____________
2. ____________
3. ____________
4. ____________
5. ____________

Hotel: ____________

1. ____________
2. ____________
3. ____________
4. ____________
5. ____________

Hotel: ____________

1. ____________
2. ____________
3. ____________
4. ____________
5. ____________

ROAD TRIP

STRETCH #:

DATE:

TO:

STARTING POINT:

ENDING POINT:

TODAY'S DRIVER(S):

WEATHER TODAY:

MUST-SEE STOPS

- [ ]
- [ ]
- [ ]
- [ ]
- [ ]
- [ ]

ITINERARY

MORNING:

AFTERNOON:

NIGHT:

What was our first impression of one of today's stops and how did it change by the time we left?

What were we most excited to see at one of today's stops and did it end up being our favorite part?

What was the best interaction we had with a stranger?

TRAVEL NOTES

LICENSE PLATE LOOKOUT

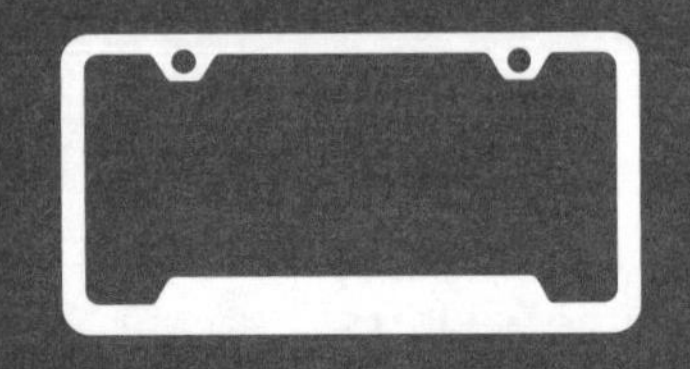

If you saw a license plate that said "RDTRP," you could be pretty confident that the car owner loves a long drive. But what if you saw a plate that said "L42CD88"? Would you be just as confident that the driver was "Linda, 42, who has 88 Cats and Dogs"? Or maybe "Larry who has 42 Compact Discs from 1988"? In this game, every license plate is a vanity plate. Take turns pointing out random license plates and trying to come up with your own explanations for what the acronyms might mean.

DATE:

Plate: ________ What it could mean: ________

Plate: ________ What it could mean: ________

Plate: ________ What it could mean: ________

Plate: ________ What it could mean: ________

Plate: ________ What it could mean: ________

Plate: ________ What it could mean: ________

Plate: ________ What it could mean: ________

Plate: ________ What it could mean: ________

Plate: ________ What it could mean: ________

Plate: ________ What it could mean: ________

DATE:

ROAD TRIP TRIVIA

How well do you know the US? Test your knowledge with some fun road trip trivia.

1. What year was Route 66 established?
   - A. 1918
   - B. 1926
   - C. 1942
   - D. 1960

2. What was the first official national park?
   - A. Yellowstone National Park
   - B. Yosemite National Park
   - C. Sequoia National Park
   - D. Glacier National Park

3. Which US city has the largest number of hotel rooms?
   - A. New York City
   - B. Orlando
   - C. Las Vegas
   - D. Los Angeles

4. What US attraction gets the most visitors every year?
   - A. Disney World
   - B. Times Square
   - C. Fisherman's Wharf
   - D. Golden Gate Bridge

5. What state is the Grand Canyon in?
   - A. Nevada
   - B. New Mexico
   - C. Utah
   - D. Arizona

6. What state is known as the "Crossroads of America"?
   - A. Indiana
   - B. Ohio
   - C. Missouri
   - D. Pennsylvania

7. What is the smallest US state by land size?
   - A. Delaware
   - B. Vermont
   - C. New Jersey
   - D. Rhode Island

8. Kringle is the official state pastry of what US state?
   - A. Illinois
   - B. Minnesota
   - C. South Carolina
   - D. Wisconsin

Answers: 1: b, 2: a, 3: c, 4: b, 5: d, 6: a, 7: d, 8: d

ROAD TRIP

STRETCH #:

DATE:

TO:

STARTING POINT:

ENDING POINT:

TODAY'S DRIVER(S):

WEATHER TODAY:

MUST-SEE STOPS

☐

☐

☐

☐

☐

☐

ITINERARY

MORNING:

AFTERNOON:

NIGHT:

What was our first impression of one of today's stops and how did it change by the time we left?

What were we most excited to see at one of today's stops and did it end up being our favorite part?

What's the best outdoor activity we did on this trip?

TRAVEL NOTES

GENERATE A ROADSIDE ATTRACTION

Is the car ride stressful right now? Try this game that's sure to lighten the mood. Have each passenger match up their birth month and first and last name with the lists to come up with a wacky roadside attraction.

DATE:

Birth Month: 1: World's Largest, 2: Statue of a, 3: Giant, 4: World's Tallest, 5: Museum of, 6: World's Smallest, 7: Big, 8: World's Ugliest, 9: Miniature, 10: World's Prettiest, 11: World's Oldest, 12: Teeny Tiny

First Letter of Your First Name: A: Shiny, B: Hissing, C: Jolly, D: Cuddly, E: Animatronic, F: Venomous, G: Makeshift, H: Ordinary, I: Embarrassing, J: Puffy, K: Talking, L: Spooky, M: Enchanted, N: Furry, O: Dazzling, P: Imaginary, Q: Brown-Eyed, R: Real, S: Hungry, T: Delicate, U: Haunted, V: Magical, W: Fancy, X: Slimy, Y: Nondescript, Z: Creepy

Last Letter of Your Last Name: A: Capybara, B: Pomegranate, C: Brussels Sprout, D: Alpaca, E: Knee Socks, F: Eggplant, G: Unicorn, H: Basset Hound, I: Pair of Pants, J: Coffee Cup, K: Avocado, L: Tuna Fish, M: Bar of Soap, N: Porcupine, O: Tennis Racket, P: Aardvark, Q: Spatula, R: Croissant, S: Flip-Flop, T: Woodpecker, U: Bow Tie, V: Cucumber, W: Gerbil, X: Sunglasses, Y: Labradoodle, Z: Lima Bean

Name: ______________________

Roadside Attraction: ______________________

Name: ______________________

Roadside Attraction: ______________________

Name: ______________________

Roadside Attraction: ______________________

Name: ______________________

Roadside Attraction: ______________________

DATE:

DESERT ISLAND

If your GPS did you wrong and you accidentally ended up stranded on a desert island, what is the one thing you'd wish you had with you? It could be something to keep you safe and secure, something to keep you entertained, or something that could help get you out of there and on your way home. Fill in your answer first and then let everyone else do the same.

Name:

Item:

Why:

Name:

Item:

Why:

Name:

Item:

Why:

Name:

Item:

Why:

Name:

Item:

Why:

Name:

Item:

Why:

ROAD TRIP

STRETCH #:

DATE:

TO:

STARTING POINT:

ENDING POINT:

TODAY'S DRIVER(S):

WEATHER TODAY:

MUST-SEE STOPS

- ☐
- ☐
- ☐
- ☐
- ☐
- ☐

ITINERARY

MORNING:

AFTERNOON:

NIGHT:

What was our first impression of one of today's stops and how did it change by the time we left?

What were we most excited to see at one of today's stops and did it end up being our favorite part?

What is something we saw that we want to learn more about? Why?

TRAVEL NOTES

FILL-IN-THE-BLANKS ROAD TRIP STORY

DATE:

Relive a favorite childhood activity with this silly, personalized storytelling game. First, fill in the blank spaces with an appropriate (or not-so-appropriate) word. Then plug your words into the story to find out what kind of adventure you had!

1. Adjective: ________
2. City: ________
3. Noun: ________
4. Number: ________
5. Adjective: ________
6. Music Genre: ________
7. Car Make/Model: ________
8. Adjective: ________
9. Adverb: ________
10. Fruit: ________
11. Animal: ________
12. Action Verb: ________
13. Snack: ________
14. Fast Food: ________
15. Hotel Chain: ________
16. Noun: ________
17. Number: ________
18. Color: ________
19. Emotion: ________
20. Adjective: ________
21. Adjective: ________
22. Action Verb: ________

Fasten your seat belts—it's time for a (1) ________ road trip! Pack your bags because we are headed to (2) ________. (And don't forget to pack your (3) ________ —you'll need it!) The drive is (4) ________ miles long and very (5) ________ so we are going to blast (6) ________ music from our (7) ________ and make lots of (8) ________ stops along the way. We'll drive (9) ________ and stop at a roadside farm to pick (10) ________ and pet some (11) ________. We'll (12) ________ to a travel center to eat our favorite (13) ________ and (14) ________. And we'll spend the night at a (15) ________. Finally, we made it to our destination: the world's largest (16) ________! It is (17) ________ feet tall and is painted (18) ________. It felt very (19) ________ to see it in person. It is very (20) ________! We had so much fun on this (21) ________ road trip, but now it is time to (22) ________ to our next destination!

LOCAL FOOD TASTE-TEST

DATE:

A road trip is the perfect time to try a food you've never tried before. There are so many opportunities to pick up a local snack at a travel center or order a regional delicacy at a roadside diner. Instead of reaching for the same old bag of potato chips or double cheeseburger, why not taste-test something that is new to you? Try some beignets, buckeyes, boiled peanuts, or Beaver Nuggets. Pick up something unique at every stop or in every state, give it a taste, and record your thoughts on this page.

Item:

State:

Rating: ☆ ☆ ☆ ☆ ☆

Notes:

Item:

State:

Rating: ☆ ☆ ☆ ☆ ☆

Notes:

Item:

State:

Rating: ☆ ☆ ☆ ☆ ☆

Notes:

Item:

State:

Rating: ☆ ☆ ☆ ☆ ☆

Notes:

ROAD TRIP

STRETCH #:

DATE:

TO:

STARTING POINT:

ENDING POINT:

TODAY'S DRIVER(S):

WEATHER TODAY:

MUST-SEE STOPS

- [ ]
- [ ]
- [ ]
- [ ]
- [ ]
- [ ]

ITINERARY

MORNING:

AFTERNOON:

NIGHT:

What was our first impression of one of today's stops and how did it change by the time we left?

What were we most excited to see at one of today's stops and did it end up being our favorite part?

What is one thing we did or want to do that is out of the ordinary?

TRAVEL NOTES

WHILE YOU WERE NAPPING

DATE:

Sometimes road trips involve long stretches of time with no stops, an ever-repeating landscape of cornfields, and the same song playing for the fifth time since you left. Inevitably, someone is going to fall asleep in the car. This is the perfect time to play a harmless prank. Come up with a story about something crazy that your dozed-off friend missed while they were napping. Say you saw a celebrity who waved as he passed by in his red Lamborghini, or that a turned-over truck spilled barbecue potato chips all over the road. The more elaborate the story and the more weird details you can add, the better. Try to convince your sleepy friend that this too-good-to-be-true story actually happened.

Who fell asleep?

What story did you tell?

DRAW WHAT YOU SAW

Pick something fun that everyone saw today on your road trip: a world's largest thing, a vintage sign, an oversized RV, a funky building, or a famed national monument. Have everyone try to draw their own artistic rendition of that thing. Give awards to whoever has the closest, furthest off, and most unique rendering.

DATE:

ROAD TRIP

STRETCH #:

DATE:

TO:

STARTING POINT:

ENDING POINT:

TODAY'S DRIVER(S):

WEATHER TODAY:

MUST-SEE STOPS

- [ ]
- [ ]
- [ ]
- [ ]
- [ ]
- [ ]

ITINERARY

MORNING:

AFTERNOON:

NIGHT:

What was our first impression of one of today's stops and how did it change by the time we left?

What were we most excited to see at one of today's stops and did it end up being our favorite part?

What has surprised us the most about this road trip?

TRAVEL NOTES

SODA FOUNTAIN CREATIONS

DATE:

An extra-large caffeinated drink in the car's cup holder is a must-have for fueling your road trip. But why settle for a simple Coke or Mountain Dew when gas stations and travel centers have walls of soda and slushie fountains filled with endless beverage choices. It's the perfect time to merge different flavors into a brand-new combo, be it Cherry Coke and root beer or grape soda and Dr Pepper. Mix it up and rate your mixture here.

Combo:

Notes:

Rating: ☆☆☆☆☆

Combo:

Notes:

Rating: ☆☆☆☆☆

Combo:

Notes:

Rating: ☆☆☆☆☆

Combo:

Notes:

Rating: ☆☆☆☆☆

Combo:

Notes:

Rating: ☆☆☆☆☆

Combo:

Notes:

Rating: ☆☆☆☆☆

ROAD PATTERNS

Often on long trips, you'll notice patterns start to form. You'll observe the same car everywhere, hear the same song on the radio again and again, and, if you're driving through the Midwest, see cornfields and cows at every turn. Pay attention to those particular patterns that form throughout your trip. Take a moment to reflect on what they mean and how they helped define your journey.

DATE:

COLOR:

FOOD:

SONG:

CARS:

SCENERY:

ROAD TRIP

STRETCH #:

DATE:

TO:

STARTING POINT:

ENDING POINT:

TODAY'S DRIVER(S):

WEATHER TODAY:

MUST-SEE STOPS

☐

☐

☐

☐

☐

☐

ITINERARY

MORNING:

AFTERNOON:

NIGHT:

What was our first impression of one of today's stops and how did it change by the time we left?

What were we most excited to see at one of today's stops and did it end up being our favorite part?

What have we celebrated on this trip? Any big occasions or small feats?

TRAVEL NOTES

FOUR-COURSE
DRIVE-THROUGH MEAL

DATE:

If your group can never decide whether to pull over for hamburgers or tacos, this game is for you. Why limit yourself to just one drive-through when you can stop at them all? Put together a multicourse drive-through meal by letting everyone in the car choose a different item from a different drive-through. Have one passenger choose where to get appetizers, a second choose entrées, a third choose a dessert, and a fourth choose a drink, all from entirely different chains. Eat an ongoing meal throughout the day, or gather up all your takeout bags at once and have a feast in your hotel room.

APPETIZER

Player: ______

Item: ______

______

From: ______

ENTRÉE

Player: ______

Item: ______

______

From: ______

DESSERT

Player: ______

Item: ______

______

From: ______

DRINK

Player: ______

Item: ______

______

From: ______

R is for having a ridiculously rad time on your road trip. Express how you're feeling about your road trip by turning it into an acrostic poem. Using each of the letters in ROAD TRIP to define the starting word of a line, write a phrase about your journey and see how it all comes together. Can't get enough? Start over using the letters in your names or the name of your destination!

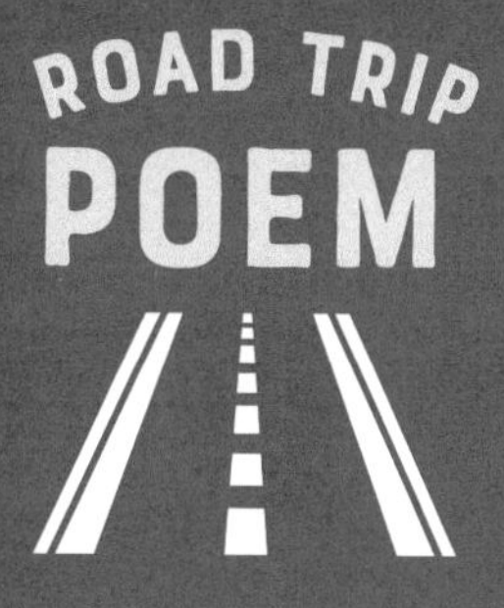

DATE:

R

O

A

D

T

R

I

P

ROAD TRIP

STRETCH #:

DATE:

TO:

STARTING POINT:

ENDING POINT:

TODAY'S DRIVER(S):

WEATHER TODAY:

MUST-SEE STOPS

- ☐
- ☐
- ☐
- ☐
- ☐
- ☐

ITINERARY

MORNING:

AFTERNOON:

NIGHT:

What was our first impression of one of today's stops and how did it change by the time we left?

What were we most excited to see at one of today's stops and did it end up being our favorite part?

What did we splurge on that was worth it?

TRAVEL NOTES

WHAT WOULD YOU SPEND IT ON?

If someone gave your group $1 to spend on your road trip, what would you buy? What if they gave you $1,000? The goal of this game is to quickly come up with one thing that would enhance your trip and would roughly be covered by the amount in question. It could be a physical object, an excursion, an upgrade, or an experience. Pull out your metaphorical wallet and get spending.

DATE:

$1 ______

$10 ______

$50 ______

$100 ______

$500 ______

$1,000 ______

$5,000 ______

$10,000 ______

DATE:

LUGGAGE TREASURE HUNT

Are you a minimalist or a chronic overpacker? In this game, the more stuff you crammed in your bags, the better your odds to win. At your accommodations, gather everyone together with all your luggage by your sides. Take turns calling out a suggestion for something everyone might have packed. It could be something obvious, like "a tube of toothpaste," or something more vague, like "a blue article of clothing." Set a timer for fifteen seconds and have everyone rummage through their bags to find an object that fits the category. If you can't find something that works, you're out. The last person standing wins.

Use these prompts or make up your own:

- Sunglasses
- Something purple
- Something that begins with the letter S
- Something you wear on your head
- An item that serves a dual purpose
- Something shiny
- Something you put in your mouth
- Something made of paper
- Something you sleep with
- Something you use in the shower

Winner: ______________________

ROAD TRIP

STRETCH #:

DATE:

TO:

STARTING POINT:

ENDING POINT:

TODAY'S DRIVER(S):

WEATHER TODAY:

MUST-SEE STOPS

- ☐
- ☐
- ☐
- ☐
- ☐
- ☐

ITINERARY

MORNING:

AFTERNOON:

NIGHT:

What was our first impression of one of today's stops and how did it change by the time we left?

What were we most excited to see at one of today's stops and did it end up being our favorite part?

What's the best indoor activity we did on this trip?

TRAVEL NOTES

TOP FIVE

What are your favorite things in the world? How do they compare with those of your travel companions? Have each person in the car go through each category and list their top fives, then compare to see what you all have in common and what you don't!

DATE:

	NAME:	NAME:	NAME:	NAME:
BOOK				
BAND/ SINGER				
TV SHOW				
MOVIE				
CITY				
MEAL				

THE ALPHABET GAME

A B C D-rive. The Alphabet Game is a fun way to pass the time on long stretches in the car. Take turns picking categories, then go through the alphabet letter by letter and think of a word that fits the theme. Your goal is to make it all the way from A to Z without getting stumped. For example, if the category was Road Trip Terms, you might say "Accelerate," "Backseat Driver," "Carpool," "Dead End," and so on, all the way to "Zebra Crossing." Choose categories from the list on this page—or come up with your own, based on your trip or interests.

DATE:

- ☐ Road Trip Terms
- ☐ Reality TV Shows
- ☐ 1990s Song Titles
- ☐ Chain Restaurants
- ☐ Things You Find in a Hotel
- ☐ Car Makes/Models/Types
- ☐ Animals
- ☐ Cities
- ☐ ______
- ☐ ______
- ☐ ______
- ☐ ______
- ☐ ______
- ☐ ______
- ☐ ______

ROAD TRIP

STRETCH #: DATE:

TO:

STARTING POINT: ENDING POINT:

TODAY'S DRIVER(S):

WEATHER TODAY:

MUST-SEE STOPS

- [ ]
- [ ]
- [ ]
- [ ]
- [ ]
- [ ]

ITINERARY

MORNING:

AFTERNOON:

NIGHT:

What was our first impression of one of today's stops and how did it change by the time we left?

What were we most excited to see at one of today's stops and did it end up being our favorite part?

What is something that challenged us on this road trip? How did we deal with it?

TRAVEL NOTES

JUST THE FACTS

DATE:

Road trips are all about learning new things. Historical sites take us to the past, museums teach us things we never knew about, and every attraction has a backstory. What fun facts did you learn on your road trip? Keep track of them here.

Fun Fact #1

Fun Fact #2

Fun Fact #3

Fun Fact #4

Fun Fact #5

Fun Fact #6

Fun Fact #7

Fun Fact #8

Fun Fact #9

Fun Fact #10

DATE:

ROAD TRIP

BUCKET LIST

What's on your group's road trip bucket list? The things you most want to see, feel, taste, or experience on the road? Do you want to drive through all forty-eight contiguous states in a row? Visit every national park? Attend a game at every MLB ballpark? Share what would make up your ultimate road trip, and then make it happen on this trip or beyond.

WE WANT TO VISIT

WE WANT TO SEE

WE WANT TO EAT

WE WANT TO STAY AT

WE WANT TO PHOTOGRAPH

WE WANT TO EXPERIENCE

WE WANT TO HEAR

ROAD TRIP

STRETCH #:

DATE:

TO:

STARTING POINT:

ENDING POINT:

TODAY'S DRIVER(S):

WEATHER TODAY:

MUST-SEE STOPS

☐

☐

☐

☐

☐

☐

ITINERARY

MORNING:

AFTERNOON:

NIGHT:

What was our first impression of one of today's stops and how did it change by the time we left?

What were we most excited to see at one of today's stops and did it end up being our favorite part?

What was our favorite mundane moment of the trip?

TRAVEL NOTES

PORTRAIT GALLERY

DATE:

After spending days in the car with your friends, you surely could remember every feature of their faces in detail, right? Take turns drawing portraits of one of your road trip companions (be sure to split it up so everyone gets drawn). The twist: You're not allowed to look at them while you do it. Have a portrait gallery showing at the end and admire how true to life or far off you are.

ODD COLOR

White, black, silver: You're going to see a lot of cars in those colors on the road. But how often do you see a pink car? Or yellow? Or orange? Decide on an obscure-for-cars color and keep track of how many vehicles you see sporting it.

DATE:

Color: ______ Tally: ______

Special details: ______

Color: ______ Tally: ______

Special details: ______

Color: ______ Tally: ______

Special details: ______

Color: ______ Tally: ______

Special details: ______

Color: ______ Tally: ______

Special details: ______

Color: ______ Tally: ______

Special details: ______

Color: ______ Tally: ______

Special details: ______

ROAD TRIP

STRETCH #:

DATE:

TO:

STARTING POINT:

ENDING POINT:

TODAY'S DRIVER(S):

WEATHER TODAY:

MUST-SEE STOPS

☐

☐

☐

☐

☐

☐

ITINERARY

MORNING:

AFTERNOON:

NIGHT:

What was our first impression of one of today's stops and how did it change by the time we left?

What were we most excited to see at one of today's stops and did it end up being our favorite part?

What do we think travel could look like in the future?

TRAVEL NOTES

FICTIONAL FAMILIES

DATE:

Do you ever wonder what *other* people are doing on their road trips? Where they're going, who they're going with, where they're staying, and so on? Look out your car windows and find other interesting-looking cars: a giant brown RV with polka-dot curtains on the windows, a beat-up sedan with an "aliens live among us" bumper sticker, an oversized minivan with four dogs in the back seat. Make up stories about the people in the car. Be as creative as you want as you imagine their backstories and tales of their travels.

Vehicle: ______________________________

Story: ______________________________

____

____

Vehicle: ______________________________

Story: ______________________________

____

____

Vehicle: ______________________________

Story: ______________________________

____

____

HUMAN JUKEBOX

DATE:

Human Jukebox is the perfect game for music lovers and wannabe a cappella stars. Start with one person singing a few lines of any song they want. The next person picks up using the last word the first person said. That person has to start singing a new song that begins with that last word. And when they are done, the next person starts singing a whole new song that starts on the last word of that song. Keep the musical chain going for as long as you can! And when you can't? Start fresh with a brand-new round. Keep track of all the songs you sang here:

ROUND ONE

ROUND TWO

ROUND THREE

ROUND FOUR

ROAD TRIP

STRETCH #:

DATE:

TO:

STARTING POINT:

ENDING POINT:

TODAY'S DRIVER(S):

WEATHER TODAY:

MUST-SEE STOPS

- ☐
- ☐
- ☐
- ☐
- ☐
- ☐

ITINERARY

MORNING:

AFTERNOON:

NIGHT:

What was our first impression of one of today's stops and how did it change by the time we left?

What were we most excited to see at one of today's stops and did it end up being our favorite part?

What unique animals or plants did we see on this trip?

TRAVEL NOTES

JACKALOPE

DATE:

If you've been driving for a long time, you've probably seen your fair share of animals on the side of the road. Birds, cows, buffalo, deer, maybe even an armadillo or bear. But have you ever seen a jackalope? Originating from Wyoming, the jackalope is a strange creature that has the body of a jackrabbit with the horns of an antelope. What other strange animals would you like to come across on your trip? Think of some offbeat combinations of your own by listing two of your favorite animals and creating a special name for the new creature.

Animal One: ______________ + Animal Two: ______________

New Creature: ______________

Animal One: ______________ + Animal Two: ______________

New Creature: ______________

Animal One: ______________ + Animal Two: ______________

New Creature: ______________

Animal One: ______________ + Animal Two: ______________

New Creature: ______________

Animal One: ______________ + Animal Two: ______________

New Creature: ______________

ONE HAS TO GO

There are so many things you can see, eat, and do on a road trip that it's often hard to select which thing to choose. But what if you had to choose one of those things to never experience again? For each of the categories here, debate over which of the choices would have to go if you had to lose one for good. Feel free to add your own item. Cross out the one you've decided to leave on the side of the road.

DATE:

FAST FOOD	BREAKFAST	TRANSPORTATION
Hamburgers	Pancakes	RV
Hot Dogs	Waffles	Convertible
Pizza	French Toast	SUV
Fried Chicken	Eggs and Bacon	Motorcycle
------------	------------	------------

SIDES	ACCOMMODATIONS	STOPS
Fries	Hotels	Roadside Attractions
Onion Rings	Airbnbs	National Parks
Cheese Curds	Campsites	Travel Centers
Chips and Guac	Bed-and-Breakfasts	Scenic Overlooks
------------	------------	------------

ROAD TRIP

STRETCH #:

DATE:

TO:

STARTING POINT:

ENDING POINT:

TODAY'S DRIVER(S):

WEATHER TODAY:

MUST-SEE STOPS

- [ ]
- [ ]
- [ ]
- [ ]
- [ ]
- [ ]

ITINERARY

MORNING:

AFTERNOON:

NIGHT:

What was our first impression of one of today's stops and how did it change by the time we left?

What were we most excited to see at one of today's stops and did it end up being our favorite part?

What positive impact has this trip had on us?

TRAVEL NOTES

WOULD YOU RATHER...

DATE:

Get to know your road trip crew a little bit more with a fun game of Would You Rather. Pose scenarios and have everyone chime in with whether they'd rather do this thing or that. Start with the prompts here and then add your own.

Would you rather...

Fly or drive

Take highways or backroads

Have a set itinerary or play it by ear

Travel to the beach or the mountains

Keep the tank full or let it ride to empty

Go camping or stay in a resort

Explore a small town or a big city

Go to a drive-through or a diner

Start early or sleep in

Make a lot of stops or drive straight there

______ or ______

______ or ______

DATE:

VENDING MACHINE CHALLENGE

It's a road trip rite of passage to raid the hotel vending machines at the end of the day. With an array of chips, candies, cookies, and sodas, it's often hard to pick just one thing. So don't: Go wild and get whatever you want by making it a challenge to see who can come up with the best or most interesting combo. Set a reasonable budget or item limit, and see what kind of vending machine concoctions you can discover. Put together a new trail mix, a wacky dessert, or a sweet and salty combo. You might have never known that Cheetos mixed with M&M's or a Twinkie coated in crushed pretzels could taste so good.

Name: .... Items: ....

Name the Concoction: .... Rating: ☆ ☆ ☆ ☆ ☆

Name: .... Items: ....

Name the Concoction: .... Rating: ☆ ☆ ☆ ☆ ☆

Name: .... Items: ....

Name the Concoction: .... Rating: ☆ ☆ ☆ ☆ ☆

Name: .... Items: ....

Name the Concoction: .... Rating: ☆ ☆ ☆ ☆ ☆

Name: .... Items: ....

Name the Concoction: .... Rating: ☆ ☆ ☆ ☆ ☆

ROAD TRIP

STRETCH #:

DATE:

TO:

STARTING POINT:

ENDING POINT:

TODAY'S DRIVER(S):

WEATHER TODAY:

MUST-SEE STOPS

☐

☐

☐

☐

☐

☐

ITINERARY

MORNING:

AFTERNOON:

NIGHT:

What was our first impression of one of today's stops and how did it change by the time we left?

What were we most excited to see at one of today's stops and did it end up being our favorite part?

What cool technology have we seen on this trip?

TRAVEL NOTES

RATING MY TRAVEL COMPANION

DATE:

What makes a good travel companion? Is it someone with type A planning skills? Someone who can get you where you're going without running off the road? Or just someone who is enjoyable to be around? All in good fun, rate each other on these crucial road trip skills to see who comes out on top.

	NAME:	NAME:	NAME:	NAME:
Music Choices	/10	/10	/10	/10
Photo Skills	/10	/10	/10	/10
Sense of Direction	/10	/10	/10	/10
Packing Skills	/10	/10	/10	/10
Car Sleeping Positions	/10	/10	/10	/10
Budgeting Skills	/10	/10	/10	/10
Planning Skills	/10	/10	/10	/10
Conversation Skills	/10	/10	/10	/10
Time on Phone	/10	/10	/10	/10
Maintenance Level	/10	/10	/10	/10
Driving Skills	/10	/10	/10	/10

ON THE HOUR

Road trips can take you through an incredible range of emotions that can change at a moment's notice. One minute you're on top of the world, cruising the freeway with wind in your hair; the next minute, your hotel loses your reservation and you're stressed out. For a full day on the road, take stock of how you feel at every hour to see how your temperament transitions throughout the day.

12:00 a.m. ____________________

1:00 a.m. ____________________

2:00 a.m. ____________________

3:00 a.m. ____________________

4:00 a.m. ____________________

5:00 a.m. ____________________

6:00 a.m. ____________________

7:00 a.m. ____________________

8:00 a.m. ____________________

9:00 a.m. ____________________

10:00 a.m. ____________________

11:00 a.m. ____________________

12:00 p.m. ____________________

1:00 p.m. ____________________

2:00 p.m. ____________________

3:00 p.m. ____________________

4:00 p.m. ____________________

5:00 p.m. ____________________

6:00 p.m. ____________________

7:00 p.m. ____________________

8:00 p.m. ____________________

9:00 p.m. ____________________

10:00 p.m. ____________________

11:00 p.m. ____________________

DATE:

ROAD TRIP

STRETCH #:

DATE:

TO:

STARTING POINT:

ENDING POINT:

TODAY'S DRIVER(S):

WEATHER TODAY:

MUST-SEE STOPS

☐

☐

☐

☐

☐

☐

ITINERARY

MORNING:

AFTERNOON:

NIGHT:

What was our first impression of one of today's stops and how did it change by the time we left?

What were we most excited to see at one of today's stops and did it end up being our favorite part?

What did we miss doing that we want to go back for?

TRAVEL NOTES

IN THE DRIVER'S SEAT

Everyone has that topic that they can wax on about for hours on end. Here you've got about three minutes. Everyone should pick one topic they are passionate about—it could be something as simple as why cats are the best animals in the world, a hot take on why pineapple belongs on pizza, or an unpopular opinion on who is the best basketball player of all time. It can be any topic they want, but the more off the wall or obscure, the better. Set a timer for three minutes and let each person take their place in the driver's seat to talk about their topic, then rate their persuasiveness.

DATE:

Name: ______________________

Topic: ______________________

____

____

Rating: ☆ ☆ ☆ ☆ ☆

Name: ______________________

Topic: ______________________

____

____

Rating: ☆ ☆ ☆ ☆ ☆

Name: ______________________

Topic: ______________________

____

____

Rating: ☆ ☆ ☆ ☆ ☆

Name: ______________________

Topic: ______________________

____

____

Rating: ☆ ☆ ☆ ☆ ☆

WHICH OF THESE ROAD TRIPS HAVE YOU TAKEN?

DATE:

These time-tested, classic road trip routes and scenic byways offer breathtaking views and a fun collection of stops. How many have you driven? Have everyone put their initials beside each classic road trip they've taken to see who has put the most mileage on their odometer.

- 48 State Ultimate USA Road Trip
- Acadia Park Loop Road
- Alaska Highway
- Appalachian Trail
- Avenue of the Giants
- Beartooth Highway
- Blue Ridge Parkway
- Blues Highway (US 61)
- Border to Border (US 93)
- Cabot Trail
- Coastal Connection Scenic Byway
- Cowboy Trail
- Crowsnest Highway
- Dempster Highway
- Fundy Coastal Drive
- Going-to-the-Sun Road
- Grand Circle Road Trip
- The Great Northern (US 2)
- Great River Road
- Hana Highway
- High Road to Taos
- I-90 Cross-Country Road Trip
- Icefields Parkway
- Irish Loop
- Kancamagus Highway
- Klondike Highway
- Lake Superior Circle Tour
- Loneliest Road in America
- Majestic Mountain Loop
- Million Dollar Highway
- Natchez Trace Parkway
- Olympic Peninsula Loop
- Oregon Trail
- Outer Banks Scenic Byway
- Overseas Highway
- Pacific Coast Highway
- Points East Coastal Drive
- Road to Nowhere (US 83)
- San Juan Skyway
- Sea to Sky Highway
- Seward Highway
- Skyline Drive
- Southern Pacific (US 80)
- Texas Hill Country
- Trans-Canada Highway
- US Route 1
- US Route 66
- US Route 163
- Utah Scenic Byway 12
- Vermont Route 100
- Viking Trail

Name: __________ Total: __________ **Name:** __________ Total: __________

Name: __________ Total: __________ **Name:** __________ Total: __________

ROAD TRIP

STRETCH #:

DATE:

TO:

STARTING POINT:

ENDING POINT:

TODAY'S DRIVER(S):

WEATHER TODAY:

MUST-SEE STOPS

- ☐
- ☐
- ☐
- ☐
- ☐
- ☐

ITINERARY

MORNING:

AFTERNOON:

NIGHT:

What was our first impression of one of today's stops and how did it change by the time we left?

What were we most excited to see at one of today's stops and did it end up being our favorite part?

What part of our trip can we not wait to tell everyone at home about?

TRAVEL NOTES

LYRIC LINK

Tired of listening to the same playlist on shuffle? Create a new set of songs by choosing random words. Name a word, any word you can think of, then come together to brainstorm and suggest songs that feature that word somewhere in the title or lyrics. If you can't think of anything off the top of your heads, search for new-to-you songs. Create an original playlist based on all the music you discover and listen to it on your drive. Jot down some of your favorite songs related to certain themes here.

DATE:

WORD/THEME: ____________________

Song: ____________ Artist: ____________

Song: ____________ Artist: ____________

Song: ____________ Artist: ____________

Song: ____________ Artist: ____________

Song: ____________ Artist: ____________

WORD/THEME: ____________________

Song: ____________ Artist: ____________

Song: ____________ Artist: ____________

Song: ____________ Artist: ____________

Song: ____________ Artist: ____________

Song: ____________ Artist: ____________

CATEGORIES

How many things can you think of that start with the same letter? Take turns going through the list of prompts and naming one item that fits each and starts with your assigned letter. Set a timer and see which combination of theme/letter fills up the fastest!

DATE:

	R	O	A	D	S
Things You Pack for a Road Trip					
Things Found on a Map					
Things to Buy at a Curio Shop					
Things Found in a Car Trunk					
Things Seen on the Side of a Road					
Things at a Breakfast Buffet					
Things Found at a Campsite					

ROAD TRIP

STRETCH #:

DATE:

TO:

STARTING POINT:

ENDING POINT:

TODAY'S DRIVER(S):

WEATHER TODAY:

MUST-SEE STOPS

☐

☐

☐

☐

☐

☐

ITINERARY

MORNING:

AFTERNOON:

NIGHT:

What was our first impression of one of today's stops and how did it change by the time we left?

What were we most excited to see at one of today's stops and did it end up being our favorite part?

What is a moment from this trip we will always remember?

TRAVEL NOTES

If you could have one road trip superpower, what would it be? Would you be invisible so you can sneak into attractions without paying? Have the ability to fly to bypass rush-hour traffic? Or teleport so you don't have to drive at all? Use the first letter of your last name to choose a superpower in the following list. How would you use it for road trip good (or evil)?

ROAD TRIP SUPERPOWER

DATE:

A: Superspeed, B: Invisibility, C: Healing, D: Telekinesis, E: Time Travel, F: Mind Control, G: Control Fire, H: Erase Memory, I: Talk to Animals, J: Flight, K: Teleport, L: X-Ray Vision, M: Shapeshifting, N: Unbreakable Bones, O: Underwater Breathing, P: Slow Down Time, Q: Camouflage, R: Superstrength, S: Control Weather, T: Clone Yourself, U: Magic, V: Psychic, W: Night Vision, X: Force Fields, Y: Elasticity, Z: Truth Extraction

Name: ______________________

Superpower: ______________________

How you would use it: ______________________

____

Name: ______________________

Superpower: ______________________

How you would use it: ______________________

____

Name: ______________________

Superpower: ______________________

How you would use it: ______________________

____

Name: ______________________

Superpower: ______________________

How you would use it: ______________________

____

ONE LAST THING

DATE:

The time has come to drop everyone off, drive home, and unpack your trunk. The end of a road trip is always a little sad, so take a moment to remember some of the very last of the best times you had on your journey.

The Last City We Visited:

The Last Attraction We Saw:

The Last Place We Stayed:

The Last Stop We Made:

The Last Place We Filled Up the Tank:

The Last Thing We Ate:

The Last Road Trip Game We Played:

The Last Song We Listened To:

Any Other Memories:

PART 2

Final Trip Log

In this part, you have the opportunity to recap each of your completed road trips with a quick snapshot of the journey. Record where you went, when you went, how you got there, and which stretches in Part 1 of this journal the trip corresponds to. Recall the best things you saw, ate, and experienced, and reminisce on what you'll always remember about your time on the road. Don't forget to give each expedition an overall rating—here's hoping that every road trip you take deserves five stars!

ROAD TRIP

RATING: ●●●●●

ROUTE:

PAGES: TO DATE(S):

I will always remember:

On this trip, I learned:

Best Thing I…

Saw:

Ate:

Experienced:

ROAD TRIP

RATING: ●●●●●

ROUTE:

PAGES: TO DATE(S):

I will always remember:

On this trip, I learned:

Best Thing I…

Saw:

Ate:

Experienced:

ROAD TRIP

RATING: ●●●●●

ROUTE:

PAGES: TO DATE(S):

I will always remember:

On this trip, I learned:

Best Thing I…

Saw:

Ate:

Experienced:

ROAD TRIP

RATING: ●●●●●

ROUTE:

PAGES: TO DATE(S):

I will always remember:

On this trip, I learned:

Best Thing I…

Saw:

Ate:

Experienced:

ROAD TRIP

RATING: ●●●●●

ROUTE:

PAGES: TO DATE(S):

I will always remember:

On this trip, I learned:

Best Thing I…

Saw:

Ate:

Experienced:

ROAD TRIP

RATING: ●●●●●

ROUTE:

PAGES: TO DATE(S):

I will always remember:

On this trip, I learned:

Best Thing I…

Saw:

Ate:

Experienced:

ROAD TRIP

RATING: ●●●●●

ROUTE:

PAGES: TO DATE(S):

I will always remember:

On this trip, I learned:

Best Thing I…

Saw:

Ate:

Experienced:

ROAD TRIP

RATING: ●●●●●

ROUTE:

PAGES: TO DATE(S):

I will always remember:

On this trip, I learned:

Best Thing I…

Saw:

Ate:

Experienced:

ROAD TRIP

RATING: ●●●●●

ROUTE:

PAGES: TO DATE(S):

I will always remember:

On this trip, I learned:

Best Thing I...

Saw:

Ate:

Experienced:

ROAD TRIP

RATING: ●●●●●

ROUTE:

PAGES: TO DATE(S):

I will always remember:

On this trip, I learned:

Best Thing I...

Saw:

Ate:

Experienced:

ROAD TRIP

RATING: ●●●●●

ROUTE:

PAGES: TO DATE(S):

I will always remember:

On this trip, I learned:

Best Thing I...

Saw:

Ate:

Experienced:

ROAD TRIP

RATING: ●●●●●

ROUTE:

PAGES: TO DATE(S):

I will always remember:

On this trip, I learned:

Best Thing I...

Saw:

Ate:

Experienced:

ROAD TRIP

RATING: ●●●●●

ROUTE:

PAGES: TO DATE(S):

I will always remember:

On this trip, I learned:

Best Thing I…

Saw:

Ate:

Experienced:

ROAD TRIP

RATING: ●●●●●

ROUTE:

PAGES: TO DATE(S):

I will always remember:

On this trip, I learned:

Best Thing I…

Saw:

Ate:

Experienced:

ROAD TRIP

RATING: ●●●●●

ROUTE:

PAGES: TO DATE(S):

I will always remember:

On this trip, I learned:

Best Thing I...

Saw:

Ate:

Experienced:

ROAD TRIP

RATING: ●●●●●

ROUTE:

PAGES: TO DATE(S):

I will always remember:

On this trip, I learned:

Best Thing I...

Saw:

Ate:

Experienced:

ROAD TRIP

RATING: ●●●●●

ROUTE:

PAGES: TO DATE(S):

I will always remember:

On this trip, I learned:

Best Thing I...

Saw:

Ate:

Experienced:

ROAD TRIP

RATING: ●●●●●

ROUTE:

PAGES: TO DATE(S):

I will always remember:

On this trip, I learned:

Best Thing I...

Saw:

Ate:

Experienced:

ROAD TRIP

RATING: ●●●●●

ROUTE:

PAGES: TO DATE(S):

I will always remember:

On this trip, I learned:

Best Thing I…

Saw:

Ate:

Experienced:

ROAD TRIP

RATING: ●●●●●

ROUTE:

PAGES: TO DATE(S):

I will always remember:

On this trip, I learned:

Best Thing I…

Saw:

Ate:

Experienced:

ROAD TRIP

RATING: ●●●●●

ROUTE:

PAGES: TO DATE(S):

I will always remember:

On this trip, I learned:

Best Thing I...

Saw:

Ate:

Experienced:

ROAD TRIP

RATING: ●●●●●

ROUTE:

PAGES: TO DATE(S):

I will always remember:

On this trip, I learned:

Best Thing I...

Saw:

Ate:

Experienced:

ROAD TRIP

RATING: ●●●●●

ROUTE:

PAGES: TO DATE(S):

I will always remember:

On this trip, I learned:

Best Thing I...

Saw:

Ate:

Experienced:

ROAD TRIP

RATING: ●●●●●

ROUTE:

PAGES: TO DATE(S):

I will always remember:

On this trip, I learned:

Best Thing I...

Saw:

Ate:

Experienced:

ROAD TRIP

RATING: ●●●●●

ROUTE:

PAGES: TO DATE(S):

I will always remember:

On this trip, I learned:

Best Thing I...

Saw:

Ate:

Experienced:

ROAD TRIP

RATING: ●●●●●

ROUTE:

PAGES: TO DATE(S):

I will always remember:

On this trip, I learned:

Best Thing I...

Saw:

Ate:

Experienced:

ROAD TRIP

RATING: ●●●●●

ROUTE:

PAGES: TO DATE(S):

I will always remember:

On this trip, I learned:

Best Thing I...

Saw:

Ate:

Experienced:

ROAD TRIP

RATING: ●●●●●

ROUTE:

PAGES: TO DATE(S):

I will always remember:

On this trip, I learned:

Best Thing I...

Saw:

Ate:

Experienced:

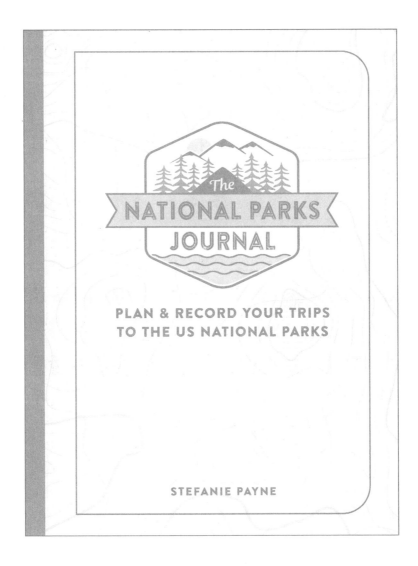